CompTIA Linux+

Last Minute Revision

Fast, Focused Revision with Real-World Fixes, Scenarios, and Exam-Style Tasks

Dorian Kelmor

GitforGits®
ASIAN PUBLISHING HOUSE

Published by: GitforGits

Publisher: Sonal Dhandre

www.gitforgits.com

Printed in India

First Printing: October 2025

ISBN: 978-93-49174-27-6

Cover Design by: Kitten Publishing

Disclaimer:

This book, including all its text, diagrams, and illustrations, is an original work developed for educational and informational purposes. The content is not affiliated with, endorsed by, or sponsored by CompTIA, or any other company, brand, or entity referenced within. All brand names, product names, and trademarks mentioned are the property of their respective owners and are used in a descriptive, educational context only. Every effort has been made to ensure that no copyrighted or trademarked material has been copied or misused in this book. All diagrams and illustrations that are not original have been used with proper attribution and credit to their respective sources.

If you believe that any content in this book infringes upon your copyright or trademark, please contact us immediately at support@gitforgits.com. Upon notification, corrective action will be taken promptly.

Prologue

Certifications are more than just milestones. They often act as turning points. For many people, the days before the CompTIA Linux+ exam are about more than just the test. It's a chance to check in, face a personal challenge, and lay the groundwork for future opportunities. In the fast-paced world of Linux system administration, where demands are always changing and time is of the essence, having a reliable reference for quick revisions is more important than ever.

The idea behind CompTIA Linux+ Last Minute Revision is simple, but it's also ambitious. It's to help you go from not knowing to feeling confident, and it does this by focusing on the most important stuff instead of going over every single topic. We made this book because we've had loads of conversations with professionals who balance complex projects, tight deadlines, and the pressure of staying current in a constantly evolving ecosystem. Each chapter has been designed with real-world needs in mind. I've met loads of candidates over the years who, even after months of studying, found themselves going back to the same stuff just days before their exam. The pattern is standard, with last-minute searches for concise problem-solving steps, practical command references, and scenario-based exercises that mirror the unpredictability of the actual exam. These stories, shared over late-night study sessions and in busy server rooms, shaped every recipe and scenario in this book.

Every section is based around the main exam subjects and is designed to help you get ready for the real thing. Instead of just listing features, it challenges you to figure out how to fix things, automate them and keep them secure, and to understand why each step is important. We've got some sample exercises and hands-on tasks that are based on situations you'd actually come across in a production environment. For example, you'll be recovering from system boot failures, fine-tuning storage, orchestrating users and permissions, securing endpoints and troubleshooting networks. In the automation chapters, you'll get hands-on with scripting solutions that make daily operations more efficient and reliable, while the cloud and containerisation sections chat about how things are deployed in a modern world.

The book basically says that to do well in the CompTIA Linux+ exam, you need to know more than just the options and commands. It's all about understanding the "how" and "why" behind every decision. The idea is to get you ready for the test and for everything that comes after, where critical thinking and technical skills are key.

"I really appreciate you trusting this book as your final revision partner. Even if this is your first certification, or the next one in a long row, I hope you go into your exam with the confidence and calmness that come from really putting in the preparation."

- Dorian Kelmor

Content

Preface

For those of you who need to get ready for your CompTIA Linux+ exam in a hurry, this book is exactly what you need. This book's got a bunch of practical tasks and focused revision to help you feel ready for your test. Every chapter is based around exam objectives and covers essential skills through step-by-step, scenario-based activities. You'll be working on recovering systems from GRUB prompts, fixing bootloader issues, and managing kernel modules. All the essential tasks, like handling file systems, logical volumes, RAID arrays and NFS mounts, are broken down into clear, easy-to-follow recipes.

There'll be plenty of practice in user and group management, permissions, access control lists and troubleshooting login and authentication issues. It covers automation techniques with Bash and Python, helping you script daily operations and validate system states. There are some great practical activities that will take you through repairing repositories, managing packages and system updates, so you'll be all set to handle real-world Linux administration. Topics like networking, service management, firewall configuration and DNS troubleshooting are taught through hands-on exercises. The security section covers things like account hygiene, SELinux and AppArmor controls, and key audit tasks. It covers modern infrastructure skills too, with hands-on chapters on containers, virtualisation, Ansible, Git, and cloud-init for automated provisioning.

Every chapter ends with some practice questions that are based on the sort of stuff you might be asked in the CompTIA Linux+ exam, and the book finishes with two full mock exams to help you work out how ready you are.

In this book you will learn to:

- Use GRUB, initramfs and kernel options to get your broken boots back up and running in no time.
- Manage your file systems, LVM and RAID without losing any data.
- Protect your users by using modes, ACLs, sudo rules and PAM sanity checks.
- Fix networks quickly: we'll clear up routes, DNS, firewalls and port conflicts for you.
- Take control of your packages and repos, pin versions, and roll back with ease and confidence.
- Script fixes that are idempotent using Bash and tiny Python helpers
- Automate with Ansible and Git so you can make changes, then keep track of them and make sure everything's above board.
- Build and debug containers, map storage, and verify cloud-init on VMs
- Spot bottlenecks fast with top, vmstat, iostat, ss, and lightweight checks.
- Test out your exam skills with chapter quizzes and two full mock tests.

GitforGits

Prerequisites

You'll probably be fine to sit this exam as long as you've used a Linux system before.

Codes Usage

Are you in need of some helpful code examples to assist you in your programming and documentation? Look no further! Our book offers a wealth of supplemental material, including code examples and exercises.

Not only is this book here to aid you in getting your job done, but you have our permission to use the example code in your programs and documentation. However, please note that if you are reproducing a significant portion of the code, we do require you to contact us for permission.

But don't worry, using several chunks of code from this book in your program or answering a question by citing our book and quoting example code does not require permission. But if you do choose to give credit, an attribution typically includes the title, author, publisher, and ISBN. For example, "CompTIA Linux+ Last Minute Revision by Dorian Kelmor".

If you are unsure whether your intended use of the code examples falls under fair use or the permissions outlined above, please do not hesitate to reach out to us at support@gitforgits.com.

We are happy to assist and clarify any concerns.

Acknowledgement

I owe a tremendous debt of gratitude to GitforGits, for their unflagging enthusiasm and wise counsel throughout the entire process of writing this book. Their knowledge and careful editing helped make sure the piece was useful for people of all reading levels and comprehension skills. In addition, I'd like to thank everyone involved in the publishing process for their efforts in making this book a reality. Their efforts, from copyediting to advertising, made the project what it is today.

Finally, I'd like to express my gratitude to everyone who has shown me unconditional love and encouragement throughout my life. Their support was crucial to the completion of this book. I appreciate your help with this endeavour and your continued interest in my career.

About Linux+ (V8) Exam

The Linux+ V8 exam measures practical competence in managing, securing, automating, and troubleshooting Linux systems — including modern cloud and hybrid environments. It validates that a professional can handle real-world Linux administration demands, and is designed for roles such as Linux Systems Administrator, Systems Engineer, or Network Engineer. The official objectives of Linux+ V8 (New Version) documented by CompTIA is available at official CompTIA+ website.

Exam Snapshot:

Exam Code: XK0-006

Total Questions: Up to 90 (includes both multiple-choice and performance-based items)

Time Allowed: 90 minutes

Passing Score: 720 (on a 100–900 scale)

Recommended Background: Approximately one year of hands-on Linux experience; prior certification such as A+, Network+, or Server+ (or equivalent knowledge) is often recommended.

This exam is ISO-certified under the ANSI National Accreditation Board standard.

Core Skill Domains:

The exam distributes emphasis across multiple domains. Percentages below reflect approximate distribution:

Domain	Approximate Weight
System Management	23%
Services & User Management	20%
Security	18%
Automation, Orchestration & Scripting	17%
Troubleshooting	22%

What You Must Know?

- System Management
  * Understand boot process, kernel fundamentals, filesystems, system architecture.
  * Manage hardware devices and kernel modules; perform storage setup and maintenance including LVM, RAID, partitions, and mounted storage.
  * Configure networks including host naming, DNS, interfaces; use essential shell and file-manipulation tools; perform backup and restore.

* Work with virtualization: create and manage virtual machines and disk images.

- Services & User Management
  * Manage file permissions, special files, links; create or manage users and groups.
  * Control processes: monitoring, priority changes, job scheduling.
  * Install, update, manage packages and repositories; manage service lifecycles, logging, and timers.
  * Operate container runtimes, manage images and container networking.
- Security
  * Configure authentication and accounting mechanisms: PAM, LDAP/Kerberos where needed; enable auditing.
  * Manage firewall rules (iptables, nftables, UFW, zone-based rules), remote access controls, sudo policies, password policies, multi-factor or advanced authentication where applicable.
  * Use cryptographic tools to manage certificates, hashing, file encryption; enforce hardening practices and maintain compliance standards.
- Automation, Orchestration & Scripting
  * Automate routine administration and operational tasks using shell scripting or Python.
  * Use configuration-management or orchestration tools (Ansible, Puppet, etc.) where applicable.
  * Maintain version control workflows, script logic, and reproducible builds; apply infrastructure-as-code style practices, and where relevant, integrate with emerging automation/AI-driven methodologies.
- Troubleshooting
  * Diagnose and resolve issues across system boot, storage, services, networking, security, and performance domains.
  * Monitor system health, logs and events; analyze CPU/memory I/O / network / resource bottlenecks.
  * Restore system stability and recover from failures with minimal downtime and maximum reliability.

Chapter 1: Boot Rescue and Service Startup

Recovering from GRUB Prompt

It was 01:15 and the hum of the data centre was audible in the background. They had a billing portal that was a pretty simple two-node setup behind a load balancer, and it had been handling all the users without any problems for months. Both VM-1 and VM-2 were sat comfortably beneath automated balance logic that checked their health and how long it took to respond. When users logged in, they just saw a familiar login page and dashboard. For the ops and security teams, this was the junction for sensitive account data, payment routines and audit streams. The maintenance window, which was circled on calendars weeks in advance, was designed for routine stability. It included cumulative OS patches, a kernel update and a simple reboot for VM-1 after nearly six weeks of steady uptime. The VM-2 would handle user traffic for this short cycle. With light usage and technical redundancy in place, there was no anxiety on the ops side.

The clock went past the 01:15 mark. VM-1's offline. The console messages kept scrolling, then suddenly stopped, and then blinked out, leaving just the silent **`grub>`** prompt. The operating system never reached user space. The load balancer did its job, draining VM-1 and keeping the portal alive through VM-2. They were never affected. For the operations team, though, it was obvious that redundancy was gone. The whole billing portal now relies on a single node. The team leader asked for an update, compliance wanted to know about the time estimate, and the IOPS alarms on VM-2 showed the extra load. It only takes one mistake, and a quick update can turn into a business outage.

Approach to Black Screen

This kind of failure, where the system halts at a **`grub>`** prompt, often triggers a sense of urgency. The temptation, in general, is to rush into trying commands, guessing at root causes, or running generic repair tools. But such thing rarely helps and often deepens the confusion.

But a diagnostic mindset is different. So here, instead of rushing in and trying every possible fix straight away, we can just pause to treat the environment as evidence and look for clues before making changes. It doesn't matter if there's a prompt, or if a menu is missing, or if there are empty sections, we can always find a way to pull it all together. At the end of the day, we're always going to do things like:

- **So, we should start with what we already know.** The VM rebooted after a patch cycle, never made it to the OS, and stopped at GRUB.
- **Start with the smallest intervention and work up to the largest one.** First, try the manual fixes, then use the rescue boot if you really have to, and only restore from backup if we have tried everything else and it's not working.
- **Try treating outputs as witnesses.** Every command's output gives us a clue, and we never do a repair that we can't check or reverse.
- **Document along the way.** We record each step and its result for everyone to see, so that any teammate or auditor can follow what's been done.

A story like this may unfold many ways, sometimes a quick prefix correction is enough, sometimes a deeper root repair may be needed. So here, the mindset is always evidence, and not the assumption, such that the next repair builds on this one, not against it.

Smallest Path First

The whole process of figuring out what's going on always starts at the site of the incident. When you get to the GRUB prompt, the first thing you want to know is what disks, partitions and files GRUB can see. The idea is to find the **/boot** partition, figure out what kernel and **initramfs** are there, and then see if we can boot it manually.

We will try out the following commands:

```
grub> ls
(hd0) (hd0,gpt1) (hd0,gpt2) (hd0,gpt3)
grub> ls (hd0,gpt2)/
lost+found/ boot/ etc/ home/ root/ var/
grub> ls (hd0,gpt2)/boot/
grub/ vmlinuz-6.6.12 initramfs-6.6.12.img config-6.6.12
System.map-6.6.12
```

From the above, the presence of both a **vmlinuz** and an **initramfs** is a good sign. If they are missing or the tree cannot be read, this signals either a configuration mismatch or deeper disk trouble, and we will need to move to a rescue environment.

Manual Boot and Recovery

If the **/boot** files are present, then we can give a try to the least invasive fix, in which we set the prefix and root for GRUB and attempt a normal boot:

```
grub> insmod normal
grub> set prefix=(hd0,gpt2)/boot/grub
grub> set root=(hd0,gpt2)
grub> normal
```

Now here, the output is going to be very informative and helpful, such as the following output:

```
GRUB menu appears:
  * Linux 6.6.12-1
```

```
* Advanced options for Linux
```

Or we can boot directly:

```
grub> linux /boot/vmlinuz-6.6.12 root=UUID=2b1a2e3f-4c5d-6e7f-8899-a0b1c2d3e4f5 ro

grub> initrd /boot/initramfs-6.6.12.img

grub> boot
```

This will give the following output:

```
Loading Linux 6.6.12 ...

Loading initial ramdisk ...

[system boot proceeds or shows kernel panic/mount error]
```

If the system boots, we still need to fix configuration so it survives the next restart.

Controlled Rescue with Live Media

If **/boot** is missing or unreadable, or the manual boot fails, we are then required to shift to a live ISO session. But here again, the focus is going to be on the evidence like the disk layout, UUIDs, and the mount points before changing anything.

See the following sample commands:

```
$ lsblk -o NAME,SIZE,FSTYPE,UUID,MOUNTPOINT

sda   80G

     sda1 512M vfat   9B1E-2A47

     sda2   1G ext4   3ce1f6e8-9414-4d12-ae12-4a1f2b1a93a1
/boot

          sda3 79G LVM2_member  B1-VolGroup

     vg0-root 60G ext4   2b1a2e3f-4c5d-6e7f-8899-a0b1c2d3e4f5

          vg0-var  19G ext4   77c0a4f4-24c9-4a9e-9b21-
1b1f2c9a3e0d

$ blkid | sort

/dev/sda1: UUID="9B1E-2A47" TYPE="vfat" PARTLABEL="EFI"

/dev/sda2: UUID="3ce1f6e8-9414-4d12-ae12-4a1f2b1a93a1"
TYPE="ext4" PARTLABEL="boot"
```

```
/dev/mapper/vg0-root: UUID="2b1a2e3f-4c5d-6e7f-8899-
a0b1c2d3e4f5" TYPE="ext4"
```

We then mount and chroot as below:

```
$ mount /dev/mapper/vg0-root /mnt
$ mount /dev/sda2 /mnt/boot
$ mount /dev/sda1 /mnt/boot/efi
$ mount --bind /dev /mnt/dev && mount --bind /proc /mnt/proc
$ mount --bind /sys /mnt/sys && mount --bind /run /mnt/run
$ chroot /mnt /bin/bash
(chroot)#
```

'fstab' Alignment

Now here, within the chroot, the alignment of the **/etc/fstab** and the output of **blkid** is going to be of much significance.

```
(chroot)# cat /etc/fstab
UUID=2b1a2e3f-4c5d-6e7f-8899-a0b1c2d3e4ff / ext4 defaults 0 1
UUID=3ce1f6e8-9414-4d12-ae12-4a1f2b1a93a1 /boot ext4 defaults
0 2
UUID=9B1E-2A47 /boot/efi vfat umask=0077 0 1
```

We then look at the mismatch:

```
-UUID=2b1a2e3f-4c5d-6e7f-8899-a0b1c2d3e4ff / ext4 defaults 0 1
+UUID=2b1a2e3f-4c5d-6e7f-8899-a0b1c2d3e4f5 / ext4 defaults 0 1
```

After the fix, we can then save the diff for future reference.

Refreshing GRUB

We've got to build a new initramfs and rework GRUB's config. Just check out the example below.

```
(chroot)# update-initramfs -c -k all
update-initramfs: Generating /boot/initrd.img-6.6.12
W: Possible missing firmware for module: virtio_scsi
```

```
(chroot)# dracut --force
dracut: Created initramfs file /boot/initramfs-6.6.12.img with
41 modules
(chroot)# grub-install /dev/sda
Installing for x86_64-efi platform.
Installation finished. No error reported.
(chroot)# grub-mkconfig -o /boot/grub/grub.cfg
Generating grub configuration file ...
Found linux image: /boot/vmlinuz-6.6.12
Found initrd image: /boot/initramfs-6.6.12.img
done
```

Clean Boot and Service Health

Once the host reboots, we then check the target, health, and listening ports:

```
$ systemctl get-default
multi-user.target
$ systemctl is-system-running
running
$ journalctl -b -p err --no-pager | tail -n +1
(no output: no errors)
$ ss -tln | awk 'NR==1 || /:22|:80|:443/'
State  Recv-Q Send-Q Local Address:Port Peer Address:Port
LISTEN 0      128    0.0.0.0:22         0.0.0.0:*
LISTEN 0      511    0.0.0.0:80         0.0.0.0:*
LISTEN 0      511    0.0.0.0:443        0.0.0.0:*
$ curl -sS -o /dev/null -w "%{http_code}\n"
http://localhost:80/health
200
```

Rolling Back Risky Kernel Tweak

There was a bit of a hiccup at some point in the evening, after a maintenance cycle had finished, when a cluster that usually behaves in a pretty predictable way started showing signs of strain on VM-2. The backing alerts said that the finance analytics service was slow, some user sessions froze for long enough to trigger timeout logs, and the load balancer recorded intermittent delays in health checks. The operations team found that yesterday's tuning round had changed a kernel parameter linked to writeback behaviour. The sysadmin who made the change was hoping to increase throughput by implementing a more aggressive caching strategy to keep computationally intensive jobs running quickly.

But the pattern told a different story the next day. While disk flush cycles were happening, processes froze, the system backlog spiked randomly, and the theory behind it all became crystal clear. The node had got into a bit of a weird memory pattern because of the parameter change. The group decided that the best thing to do would be to roll back the change, so we wouldn't have to reinstall the operating system or do a full reboot. Once we've got safe defaults sorted, stabilised memory activity and a clear summary of the evidence, we can consider the service back to normal.

Reversal with Control

A kernel parameter rollback is a task where restraint becomes more valuable than speed alone. Once a node begins showing symptoms after a low-level change, it is tempting to dive into configuration files, repeat assumptions, or apply quick edits wherever the eye lands. A more deliberate mindset pays off quickly.

So here, we start by identifying exactly which parameter changed, so we do not risk touching anything unrelated. We create a temporary safe path to test the rollback, so we do not worsen the environment by applying persistent edits before we understand their effect. We keep a reversible escape plan, usually a second shell or an attached console, so we can recover gracefully if the active session locks up the network stack or triggers new issues. This mindset ensures that the node regains its footing without startling the live workload or introducing fresh uncertainty.

Discovering Instability

Our first practical step is to review persistent configuration files that may have been altered during tuning. Here, the two primary search areas would be the **/etc/sysctl.conf** and the directory **/etc/sysctl.d/**. These locations commonly store persistent overrides, and hence we begin by listing all non commented entries, so we can see the effective changes applied.

```
$ grep -v '^#' /etc/sysctl.conf /etc/sysctl.d/*.conf
2>/dev/null
```

```
/etc/sysctl.conf:vm.dirty_ratio=60
```

```
/etc/sysctl.d/perf.conf:kernel.sched_autogroup_enabled=1
```

At this point, we suspect that the amplified caching behavior is coming from the **vm.dirty_ratio** setting. To understand how active the change is, we ask the system for the current value.

```
$ sysctl vm.dirty_ratio
vm.dirty_ratio = 60
```

Usually, this parameter remains at a calmer value. Generally, the default is kept at 20, but let us assume it was raised to 60, probably for a more aggressive caching pattern. That increase may amplify memory pressure during flush cycles. Since the spike in stalls aligns with this adjustment, we treat it as the most likely contributor.

So here, we can try to test the rollback using a temporary change instead of touching the persistent configuration immediately.

```
$ sysctl -w vm.dirty_ratio=20
vm.dirty_ratio = 20
```

This temporary rollback helps us observe memory behavior without committing to permanent changes. If the system stabilizes, we know we are on the right track.

Otherwise, we can also scan for active writeback or memory pressure hints.

```
$ dmesg | grep -i 'writeback\|memory'
# (Either empty or containing non critical messages after
rollback)
```

Verifying Stability

Once the system begins acting normally again, we can think of taking a careful step toward making the rollback persistent.

```
$ sudo sed -i '/vm.dirty_ratio/s/^/# /' /etc/sysctl.conf
```

We then confirm the change:

```
$ sudo grep -v '^#' /etc/sysctl.conf
# (No output for vm.dirty_ratio because it is commented out)
```

After this, we then reload the settings so the persistent state matches the current runtime condition.

```
$ sudo sysctl --system
* Applying /etc/sysctl.conf ...
* Applying /etc/sysctl.d/ ...
* Setting kernel parameters ... [OK]
```

We do the checking again:

```
$ sysctl vm.dirty_ratio
vm.dirty_ratio = 20
```

This will help us to verify that the system is now running with the safe value.

Keeping Reversible Exit Plan

During any rollback involving low level parameters, it is wise to keep a second shell active. This can be a console session through the hypervisor or a multiplexed terminal through tools like **tmux**.

```
$ tmux new -s rescue
```

One pane applies the rollback while the other monitors application health.

```
$ curl -sSf http://localhost:8080/health
OK
```

This pattern protects us from being stranded if a change unexpectedly affects networking or process scheduling.

System Health Verification

This is the final step. Here, we aim to get a clear, concise evidence pack that shows everything is working normally again. This includes confirming the safe parameter, checking active health, reviewing logs, and testing service endpoints.

```
$ sysctl vm.dirty_ratio
vm.dirty_ratio = 20
$ uptime
```

```
 16:42:12 up 20 days,  5:01,  2 users,  load average: 0.07,
0.04, 0.05
$ journalctl -b -p err --no-pager | tail -n +1
(no output)
$ ss -tln | awk 'NR==1 || /:22|:8080/'
State Recv-Q Send-Q Local Address:Port Peer Address:Port
LISTEN 0      128      0.0.0.0:22      0.0.0.0:*
LISTEN 0      512      0.0.0.0:8080    0.0.0.0:*
```

Finally:

```
$ curl -sS -o /dev/null -w "%{http_code}\n"
http://localhost:8080/health
200
```

This tell us that the node is stable, the parameter is safe, and no lingering errors appear after rollback.

Overall, the kernel parameters can create remarkable improvements when tuned wisely, but they can also trigger unexpected pressure patterns when pushed too far. This recipe reinforces the same calm, evidence-based rhythm that we learned in the previous topic. It offered the same model which we can reuse whenever we see that the kernel behavior requires the quick reversible correction.

Service Reliability using Smart Unit Overrides

For the sake of this example, we'll say the compliance dashboard for the analytics group is built on a Node.js service, deployed as a systemd unit called **compliance-dashboard.service**. And, during a recent package upgrade, the team noticed the dashboard sometimes fails to start cleanly after a reboot or update. The logs show "Environment variable not set" and, less frequently, "Too many open files" errors. Sometimes, the service launches with missing dependencies, leading to incomplete data loads.

The root cause?

The **systemd** service files are generic, and subtle mismatches in environment, resource limits, or startup order keep breaking the process in unpredictable ways. We need a reliable method to override just what matters, without editing vendor files or risking config drift. The task is to create drop-in overrides for environment, limits, and dependencies so the service launches correctly every time, even after updates or full host reboots.

Pinpointing Instability

When a service fails to start, there is an urge to edit the main unit file directly, restart everything, or blame package maintainers. The smarter approach is surgical.

The questions that will come to our mind, are:

Is the service definition missing a critical environment variable or resource limit?

Does it depend on another service that sometimes isn't ready?

Does the start-up order get broken after updates or reboots?

So here, we start to review the exact failure messages and the current service status, then ask systemd what it expects versus what the environment provides. We only create overrides for the necessary parts, environment, limits, and dependencies, keeping the main package files untouched for safe upgrades later.

Investigating Current State

To begin with, we look at the status and recent logs for the target service. Here, the name is **`compliance-dashboard.service`**. The logs quickly show if missing environment variables or resource limits are the issue.

```
$ systemctl status compliance-dashboard.service

   Loaded: loaded (/lib/systemd/system/compliance-
dashboard.service; enabled)

   Active: failed (Result: exit-code) since Thu 2025-07-17
09:16:45 UTC; 2min ago

  Process: 2346 ExecStart=/usr/bin/node
/srv/dashboard/server.js (code=exited, status=1/FAILURE)

 Main PID: 2346 (code=exited, status=1/FAILURE)


Jul 17 09:16:45 dashboard-node systemd[1]: Started Compliance
Analytics Dashboard.

Jul 17 09:16:45 dashboard-node node[2346]: FATAL: Environment
variable DASHBOARD_SECRET not set

Jul 17 09:16:45 dashboard-node systemd[1]: compliance-
dashboard.service: Main process exited, code=exited,
status=1/FAILURE
```

We then check the open files limit and other resource settings, especially when errors like "Too many open files" appear in logs.

```
$ journalctl -u compliance-dashboard.service -b | grep -i
'open files'
Jul 17 09:18:10 dashboard-node node[2412]: Error: EMFILE: too
many open files
```

Also, we then check for missing dependencies:

```
$ journalctl -u compliance-dashboard.service -b | grep -i
'dependency'
# (Output shows: "Failed to connect to postgres.service")
```

Creating Drop-in Overrides

Environment Variables

The **systemd** allows us to set environment variables in a dedicated override file. We never edit **/lib/systemd/system/compliance-dashboard.service** directly. Instead, we use:

```
$ sudo systemctl edit compliance-dashboard.service
```

This opens an editor. We then add only the settings needed:

```
[Service]
Environment="DASHBOARD_SECRET=supersecretvalue"
```

After this, we then save and exit. Now, to verify:

```
$ systemctl show compliance-dashboard.service --
property=Environment
Environment=DASHBOARD_SECRET=supersecretvalue
```

Resource Limits

In case, if we want to raise the open files limit for the dashboard:

```
$ sudo systemctl edit compliance-dashboard.service
```

And then we append:

```
[Service]
LimitNOFILE=4096
```

Then, immediately we save and run the following to verify:

```
$ systemctl show compliance-dashboard.service --
property=LimitNOFILE
LimitNOFILE=4096
```

Dependencies and Ordering

If the dashboard needs Postgres to be up first, then we specify:

```
$ sudo systemctl edit compliance-dashboard.service
```

And, we add:

```
[Unit]
After=postgresql.service
Requires=postgresql.service
```

This ensures the dashboard only starts after the database is available.

Reloading and Testing Override

After changes, we then reload the systemd manager configuration and restart the service:

```
$ sudo systemctl daemon-reload
$ sudo systemctl restart compliance-dashboard.service
```

We can also check the status as below:

```
$ systemctl status compliance-dashboard.service
   Loaded: loaded (/lib/systemd/system/compliance-
dashboard.service; enabled; vendor preset: enabled)
  Drop-In: /etc/systemd/system/compliance-dashboard.service.d
     override.conf
   Active: active (running) since Thu 2025-07-17 09:29:42 UTC;
2s ago
```

```
 Main PID: 2685 (node)
    Tasks: 12 (limit: 4096)
   Memory: 41.2M
   CGroup: /system.slice/compliance-dashboard.service
     2685 /usr/bin/node /srv/dashboard/server.js
```

Functional Probe and Stability Check

After the dashboard reports as running, we then check the health endpoint and verify connections to dependencies.

```
$ curl -sS -o /dev/null -w "%{http_code}\n"
http://localhost:3000/health
200
```

Now here, to simulate a reboot or package upgrade scenario:

```
$ sudo systemctl reboot
```

After reboot, we can then immediately verify service health and overrides:

```
$ systemctl status compliance-dashboard.service | grep Active
Active: active (running) since Thu 2025-07-17 09:35:19 UTC;
1min 10s ago
$ systemctl show compliance-dashboard.service --
property=Environment --property=LimitNOFILE --property=After -
-property=Requires
Environment=DASHBOARD_SECRET=supersecretvalue
LimitNOFILE=4096
After=postgresql.service
Requires=postgresql.service
$ curl -sS -o /dev/null -w "%{http_code}\n"
http://localhost:3000/health
200
```

Overall, the smart, minimal unit overrides let us fix what is broken without risking the mess of editing vendor files. They make the service start reliably, keep it healthy through updates, and guarantee every fix is traceable. For each override, we have a targeted test and evidence that remains stable across the full lifecycle, from deployment to the next maintenance cycle.

Capturing Incident Evidence

Now here, let us think that there is a customer service portal, running on VM-2, and it failed to process requests at 11:35 this morning. The dashboard service might have dropped from the load balancer, and several application logs were rotated before the underlying cause could be reviewed.

But, the support staff need a clean, time-boxed snapshot of what went wrong, without wading through thousands of unrelated messages or risking contamination by after-the-fact system noise. So here, the task here for us is to carve out the relevant window of evidence from systemd's journal, then tie it precisely to the incident, and prepare a compact verification line that not only exposes the fault but shows how the recovery changed system behavior.

So here, the goal for us is to capture the entries that appeared from just before the incident through the fix, so anyone reviewing later can understand exactly what broke and how our work improved the state. The ideal output of such exercise is a short, targeted journal slice, followed by a single-line verifier that demonstrates the health of the system after remediation.

Carving Incident Window

So, let us begin! Since the dashboard service failed at 11:35 and was restarted successfully at 11:41, we will first retrieve the relevant time range using **journalctl** with the **--since** and **--until** flags.

```
$ journalctl -u compliance-dashboard.service --since "2025-07-17 11:30" --until "2025-07-17 11:45" --no-pager > dashboard-incident.log
```

Following is the sample output which is generally saved in **dashboard-incident.log**:

```
Jul 17 11:34:58 dashboard-node systemd[1]: Stopping Compliance Analytics Dashboard...

Jul 17 11:35:00 dashboard-node node[2911]: FATAL: Environment variable DASHBOARD_SECRET not set

Jul 17 11:35:00 dashboard-node systemd[1]: compliance-dashboard.service: Main process exited, code=exited, status=1/FAILURE

Jul 17 11:35:00 dashboard-node systemd[1]: compliance-dashboard.service: Failed with result 'exit-code'.
```

```
Jul 17 11:40:15 dashboard-node systemd[1]: Starting Compliance Analytics Dashboard...
Jul 17 11:41:08 dashboard-node systemd[1]: Started Compliance Analytics Dashboard.
Jul 17 11:41:09 dashboard-node node[3044]: Dashboard listening on port 3000
```

This above slice covers the entire incident and nothing else. It can be attached to an incident ticket, emailed to developers, or kept as an audit trail for postmortems.

Attaching Verifier

The incident evidence is only as strong as the immediate check that follows. After the service is restored, we then append a one-liner verifier to confirm the fix and show that the system is truly healthy.

So here, a health endpoint probe will be the fastest way to close the loop as below:

```
$ curl -sS -o /dev/null -w "%{http_code}\n" http://localhost:3000/health
200
```

If the output is **200**, themn we can say that the service is up. This output, together with the journal slice, tells the whole story of what broke, how it was fixed, and whether the dashboard is truly working again.

This model of compact, evidence-driven incident reporting will be the habit for every root cause in the recipes ahead.

Stabilizing Flapping Service

One of the most persistent headaches in IT operations is a service that starts and then fails repeatedly, a phenomenon known as “flapping.” This pattern emerges across environments, such as a web API that fails to bind its port, a database that times out during initialization, or a monitoring agent that launches before its dependencies are ready. Each cycle of restart and failure increases system load, floods the logs with repetitive errors, and often masks the real root cause behind a curtain of noise.

Now here, for support teams, a flapping service can trigger false alarms, disrupt failover policies, and erode trust in automation. Underneath these symptoms, the root issues often stem from a mismatch in readiness, like missing environment variables, delayed dependencies, or strict resource limits that the main process cannot satisfy at boot. So here, if we want to bring stability to such a service, then it will require a layered troubleshooting, which is followed with targeted configuration changes. This ultimately will guarantee us that the process is truly ready before **systemd** reports it as healthy.

Reproducing Flap

Firstly, we begin with forcing the flap in a controlled way so we can catch its pattern and confirm its triggers. Now here, we will make a small assumption that the **analytics-api.service** is the culprit. And, so here, a quick manual restart cycle will immediately let us know the pattern in both service status and logs.

Following is the sample script:

```
$ sudo systemctl restart analytics-api.service
$ systemctl status analytics-api.service
   Loaded: loaded (/lib/systemd/system/analytics-api.service; enabled)
   Active: activating (auto-restart) since Fri 2025-07-18 14:21:44 UTC; 3s ago
  Process: 3089 ExecStart=/usr/bin/python3 /srv/api/server.py (code=exited, status=1/FAILURE)
 Main PID: 3089 (code=exited, status=1/FAILURE)
```

We then examine at the logs, and so here we see:

```
$ journalctl -u analytics-api.service --since -10m --no-pager | grep -i 'error\|fail'
Jul 18 14:21:44 api-host python3[3089]: FATAL: Unable to bind port 8080 (Address already in use)
Jul 18 14:21:44 api-host systemd[1]: analytics-api.service: Main process exited, code=exited, status=1/FAILURE
Jul 18 14:21:44 api-host systemd[1]: analytics-api.service: Failed with result 'exit-code'.
```

If we repeatedly restart the service, the same error appears. The logs also show rapid cycling too:

```
$ journalctl -u analytics-api.service --since -1h | grep "auto-restart"
```

```
Jul 18 14:18:35 api-host systemd[1]: analytics-api.service: Service RestartSec=5s expired, scheduling restart.
Jul 18 14:18:40 api-host systemd[1]: analytics-api.service: Scheduled restart job, restart counter is at 4.
```

This overall confirms that the service is indeed flapping. It is restarting without ever reaching a healthy state.

Isolating Readiness Issues

With the symptoms captured, the next move is to pinpoint readiness issues. Now this is just for your knowledge about the common pattern, which are:

- Another process may be holding the required port.
- A database or API endpoint is unavailable at the time the service starts.
- The service tries to start before the system or its dependencies are fully ready.
- Insufficient file descriptors, memory, or CPU.

Let us consider that the log are showing a port binding failure. So just to confirm, we can check what is using the port:

```
$ ss -tlnp | grep :8080
LISTEN 0      128     0.0.0.0:8080      0.0.0.0:*
users:(("python3",pid=2967,fd=8))
```

From the above, we find that another instance of the service, or perhaps a debugging process, is still running. So now, to avoid the race, we then clean up any old process and retest.

```
$ sudo fuser -k 8080/tcp
$ sudo systemctl restart analytics-api.service
```

The status now shows the process holds the port without flapping.

```
$ systemctl status analytics-api.service
   Loaded: loaded (/lib/systemd/system/analytics-api.service; enabled)
   Active: active (running) since Fri 2025-07-18 14:26:51 UTC; 4s ago
 Main PID: 3123 (python3)
```

Adjusting Start Conditions and Dependencies

If a dependency is sometimes late (like a database), the systemd's "After" and "Requires" directives will not let the API launch until the dependencies are healthy. So here, we then add a drop-in override for dependencies:

```
$ sudo systemctl edit analytics-api.service
```

We then append to the file:

```
[Unit]
After=postgresql.service
Requires=postgresql.service
```

Now here, for slow services, we can add "RestartSec" to reduce the restart rate, and it helps the dependencies with more time to come up:

```
[Service]
RestartSec=10
```

Stability Validation

After fixing the root issue and improving dependencies, we then reload the manager configuration and restart:

```
$ sudo systemctl daemon-reload
$ sudo systemctl restart analytics-api.service
```

We can also check the status and logs again to confirm the flap is resolved:

```
$ systemctl status analytics-api.service
   Loaded: loaded (/lib/systemd/system/analytics-api.service; enabled)
   Active: active (running) since Fri 2025-07-18 14:34:19 UTC; 19s ago
 Main PID: 3152 (python3)
```

Post this, we then test the application's health endpoint:

```
$ curl -sS -o /dev/null -w "%{http_code}\n"
http://localhost:8080/health
200
```

If this result is steady over several cycles, we can be sure that the service is now stable.

Knowledge Exercise

1. A system boots to the **grub>** prompt after an update. The **/boot** partition is at **(hd0,gpt2)**. Which GRUB command sequence should you use first to attempt a manual boot using the available kernel and initramfs?

   A.

```
insmod normal
set prefix=(hd0,gpt2)/boot/grub
set root=(hd0,gpt2)
normal
```

   B.

```
insmod efi
set root=(hd0,gpt1)
boot
```

   C.

```
linux /vmlinuz root=/dev/sda2
initrd /initrd.img
boot
```

2. We mount a root filesystem in a live rescue shell and see this line in **/etc/fstab**:

```
UUID=9f00b2d8-....e2b0 / ext4 defaults 0 1
```

   Running `blkid` returns:

```
/dev/mapper/vg0-root: UUID="43be17d0-....e2b0"
```

What is the best next action?

A. Edit **/etc/fstab** to use the UUID shown by **blkid**
B. Format the root partition to match the fstab
C. Remove the fstab entry

3. Why would you run **update-initramfs -c -k all** or **dracut --force** in a chroot before rebooting after fixing a boot issue?
   A. To refresh the early userspace and include correct drivers and hooks
   B. To reinstall the operating system
   C. To remove all old kernels
4. Which device should you specify when running **grub-install** on a UEFI system with **/boot/efi** mounted at **/mnt/boot/efi**?
   A. **/dev/sda**
   B. **/mnt/boot**
   C. **/mnt/boot/efi**
5. After rebuilding the bootloader and initramfs, which output is most helpful as immediate evidence for a successful repair before rebooting?

   A.

```
ls -lh /boot/initramfs*
grep -E "linux|initrd" /boot/grub/grub.cfg
```

   B.

```
ls /tmp
ps aux
```

   C.

```
history | tail
```

6. After a successful boot, which command shows only errors from the current session?

   A.

```
journalctl -b -p err --no-pager
```

   B.

```
dmesg | tail
```

   C.

```
cat /var/log/messages
```

7. Your application exposes a health endpoint on port 8080. Which command best confirms the endpoint is alive and returns HTTP 200?

   A.

```
curl -sS -o /dev/null -w "%{http_code}\n"
http://localhost:8080/health
```

   B.

```
netstat -an
```

   C.

```
ping 127.0.0.1
```

8. While using a live ISO for repair, why are **/dev**, **/proc**, **/sys**, and **/run** mounted into the chroot environment?
   A. So system tools and commands work correctly inside chroot
   B. To make the system boot faster
   C. To increase security on the rescue host
9. After running post-repair scripts, you see:

```
systemctl is-system-running
running
ss -tln | grep 443
LISTEN 0      128    0.0.0.0:443   0.0.0.0:*
```

What does this output tell you?

   A. The system is healthy and HTTPS is listening
   B. The system has critical errors
   C. The service is stopped
10. We make a change in **/etc/fstab** and realize after a reboot the system does not mount **/boot** correctly. Which prior artifact would help us quickly recover?
   A. A saved diff of the file before the edit
   B. The output of **ls /var**
   C. The result of **ps aux**

Note: In this chapter quiz, option A is the correct answer for every question.

CHAPTER 2: FILESYSTEMS, MOUNTS, LVM AND RAID

Booting Clean After fstab Mistakes

As I said before, the maintenance window in the billing portal brought kernel and package updates, as well as a subtle change to the filesystem layout. The infrastructure team, seeking to standardize disk usage across all VMs, moved **/var** onto its own logical volume and updated the **/etc/fstab** entries on both VM-1 and VM-2. The change was meant to be seamless. But, as the dust settled after a late reboot, VM-1 failed to reach the multi-user target. The console reported boot failures, with messages about "cannot mount /var" and drops into emergency mode. The traffic continued through VM-2, yet the team was left troubleshooting a node that would not complete the boot sequence. This problem is common whenever **fstab** is edited, typos, wrong UUIDs, or missing mount options can leave even healthy filesystems unmounted, causing services to fail and manual intervention to be required. The objective is to return to a clean, predictable boot where filesystems mount as intended and errors are eliminated before the next restart.

So here, the key to recovering from **fstab** mistakes is to pause before rushing into edit cycles. Boot failures rooted in mount errors often present as dropped shells, emergency prompts, or failed services long before a user prompt ever appears. Rather than blindly editing **fstab** or removing lines, the method is to gather evidence: which devices are present, which UUIDs are correct, and what the system expects according to the current **fstab**. This diagnostic habit is about working methodically, verifying identifiers, testing manual mounts, and preparing temporary fallbacks that allow full boot without data loss. The goal is to eliminate the guesswork and replace it with clean, predictable mounts verified by the system itself.

Correcting Identifiers and Testing Mounts

At first, we start with the evidence. For this, from the emergency shell or a rescue session, we begin to collect device details and the current **fstab**:

```
$ lsblk -o NAME,SIZE,FSTYPE,UUID,MOUNTPOINT
sda     80G
     sda1 512M vfat   9B1E-2A47
     sda2   1G ext4   3ce1f6e8-9414-4d12-ae12-4a1f2b1a93a1
/boot
     sda3 10G ext4   e1d2f6f1-18b7-457a-b187-5b2e94389a2c /var
          sda4 69G LVM2_member  B1-VolGroup
               vg0-root 69G ext4   2b1a2e3f-4c5d-6e7f-8899-
a0b1c2d3e4f5 /
```

Next, we list the relevant section of **/etc/fstab**:

```
$ cat /etc/fstab
UUID=2b1a2e3f-4c5d-6e7f-8899-a0b1c2d3e4f5 /     ext4 defaults 0 1
UUID=3ce1f6e8-9414-4d12-ae12-4a1f2b1a93a1 /boot ext4 defaults 0 2
UUID=DEADBEEF-0000-0000-0000-000000000000 /var ext4 defaults 0 2
```

In the above, the **/var** references an incorrect or missing UUID. So here, we then cross-check with **lsblk** and **blkid** outputs. If the actual **/var** device is **e1d2f6f1-18b7-457a-b187-5b2e94389a2c**, we then correct the **fstab** line accordingly.

```
# Edit /etc/fstab
UUID=e1d2f6f1-18b7-457a-b187-5b2e94389a2c /var ext4 defaults 0 2
```

After this, we then test the mount manually to confirm:

```
$ mount /var
$ mount | grep /var
/dev/sda3 on /var type ext4 (rw,relatime)
```

If the mount succeeds, the identifier fix is correct.

Introducing Temporary Fallback

Now, if the system cannot resolve a new mount, or if you are unsure about the safety of mounting a volume, we here then introduce a temporary fallback. It allows the system to boot fully for further troubleshooting, rather than stalling at an emergency shell. For example, you can comment out the problem entry in **/etc/fstab** and manually mount the filesystem after boot, giving more time for a safe fix as shown below:

```
# In /etc/fstab, comment out the problem line
#UUID=e1d2f6f1-18b7-457a-b187-5b2e94389a2c /var ext4 defaults 0 2
```

Next, we then reboot and once in multi-user mode, we then mount manually:

```
$ mount /dev/sda3 /var
```

This gives us full access while we are analyzing it.

Confirming Persistent Mounts using 'findmnt'

After making changes, we then use the **findmnt** to confirm that all filesystems specified in **fstab** are present and mounted as intended.

```
$ findmnt --verify --tab-file /etc/fstab
TARGET SOURCE                  FSTYPE OPTIONS     LABEL
UUID
/      /dev/mapper/vg0-root    ext4   defaults
2b1a2e3f-...
/boot  /dev/sda2               ext4   defaults
3ce1f6e8-...
/var   /dev/sda3               ext4   defaults
e1d2f6f1-...
$ sudo reboot
```

If all mounts appear without errors, and **findmnt --verify** produces no warnings, the configuration is stable.

Then after the system comes up:

```
$ findmnt | grep -E '/$|/boot|/var'
/      /dev/mapper/vg0-root    ext4    rw,relatime
/boot  /dev/sda2               ext4    rw,relatime
/var   /dev/sda3               ext4    rw,relatime
```

With this, all targets are mounted correctly and persist across reboots.

The approach of the discipline of methodical checks, temporary workarounds, and final proof with **findmnt** guides us in preventing the emergencies before they disrupt users or critical workloads.

Growing Live Filesystem

There can be a situation wherein in one of the previous quarter, the billing application team rolled out a new reporting module that began consuming much more space in **/var/log** and **/var/reports** than anticipated. And within weeks, it came to our notice that the VM-2's

/var logical volume approached 90% usage, thereby causing nightly jobs to fail and filling monitoring dashboards with alerts.

So here, the team needed a way to expand the logical volume and filesystem while the system was live. And, the expanding of a live filesystem is a routine operation for most of the Linux administrators. Now, before making any irreversible changes, the ideal workflow is to double-check the logical volume and free space, prepare a snapshot to act as an instant rollback, expand the filesystem online, and then confirm the result with both system tools and application tests. What we want to learn here is that we want to practice zero-downtime upgrades that are visible, safe, and repeatable on any node.

Reviewing Logical Volumes and Free Space

At first, we will review the current usage and logical volume layout:

```
$ lsblk -o NAME,SIZE,FSTYPE,TYPE,MOUNTPOINT
sda           80G    ...  disk
sda1       512M    ...  part /boot
sda2        10G    ...  part
sda3        69G    ...  part
     vg0-root  50G  ext4 lvm  /
          vg0-var   19G  ext4 lvm  /var
$ df -h /var
Filesystem            Size  Used Avail Use% Mounted on
/dev/mapper/vg0-var    19G   17G  1.1G  95% /var
```

Then, we check free space in the volume group:

```
$ vgs
VG    #PV #LV #SN Attr    VSize    VFree
vg0    1   2   0 wz--n-  69.00g  10.00g
```

Here, we can see that there is 10 GB free, which is enough for a safe extension.

Creating Snapshot

Next, we now create a snapshot of the logical volume:

```
$ lvcreate --size 2G --snapshot --name var-snap vg0/vg0-var
```

```
Logical volume "var-snap" created
```

We can then check if the snapshot appears:

```
$ lvs
LV        VG    Attr        LSize  Pool Origin   Data%  Meta%
Move Log Cpy%Sync Convert
root      vg0   -wi-ao---- 50.00g
var       vg0   -wi-ao---- 19.00g
var-snap  vg0   swi-a-s---  2.00g       var        0.00
```

From the above, if anything fails after resizing, this snapshot can be rolled back to restore the state instantly.

Extending Logical Volume

We then grow the **/var** logical volume by 5 GB:

```
$ lvextend -L +5G /dev/vg0/var
Size of logical volume vg0/var changed from 19.00 GiB (4864
extents) to 24.00 GiB (6144 extents).
Logical volume vg0/var successfully resized.
```

Expanding Filesystem Online

We then resize the ext4 filesystem online, and there is no reboot needed:

```
$ resize2fs /dev/vg0/var
resize2fs 1.46.5 (30-Dec-2021)
Filesystem at /dev/vg0/var is mounted on /var; on-line
resizing required
old_desc_blocks = 3, new_desc_blocks = 4
The filesystem on /dev/vg0/var is now 6291456 (4k) blocks
long.
```

We then verify the increase:

```
$ df -h /var
```

```
Filesystem             Size  Used Avail Use% Mounted on
/dev/mapper/vg0-var     24G   17G  6.1G  74% /var
```

Validating System and App Check

We will now check if there is new space available at both the system and application level:

```
$ lsblk -o NAME,SIZE,FSTYPE,TYPE,MOUNTPOINT | grep var
vg0-var 24G ext4 lvm /var
$ df -h /var
Filesystem             Size  Used Avail Use% Mounted on
/dev/mapper/vg0-var     24G   17G  6.1G  74% /var
```

If we need to test a key application or database function that depends on /var, for example, consider writing a test file or restarting a log-consuming service:

```
$ touch /var/test_expand_success
$ ls -l /var/test_expand_success
-rw-r--r-- 1 root root 0 Jul 19 18:44 /var/test_expand_success
```

If the application or system misbehaves after expansion, revert to the snapshot:

```
$ umount /var
$ lvconvert --merge /dev/vg0/var-snap
# After merging, reboot if needed to remount cleanly
$ reboot
```

This instantly restores **/var** to its pre-expansion state with minimal risk.

Basically, by reviewing layout, taking a snapshot, expanding both the logical volume and the filesystem online, and validating changes with system and real application checks, we build habits that eliminate downtime and offer true operational safety, regardless of user demand or maintenance windows.

Shrinking Wrong-Sized LV

A few months ago, the VM-1 was provisioned with a 32 GB **/var** logical volume, far more than needed, since real use never crosses 3 GB, even at audit time. The storage pressure on the pool has risen, and the backup windows are now tight. So now, the team decides to reclaim the wasted space, but everyone remembers a past incident where a rushed LV shrink corrupted the filesystem and cost a whole day of manual restores. So, the team must plan to shrink **/var** safely with a protective snapshot, shrinking the filesystem first, and then the LV.

Before we do it, we must understand that shrinking a logical volume is not simply the reverse of expansion. It is a careful, one-way process in which we always reduce the filesystem first, and only then shrink the LV. And, each step should be paired with evidence, clean filesystem checks, validation with checksum probes, and final proof that everything works as expected. This way, even if the team is interrupted, the rollback is quite quick and no user notices anything but more available space in the pool.

Preparing Shrink

Before making any changes, we first capture the state for evidence and rollback:

```
$ df -h /var
Filesystem            Size  Used Avail Use% Mounted on
/dev/mapper/vg0-var    32G  2.6G  28G    9% /var
$ lvs
LV   VG   Attr        LSize  Pool Origin Data%  Meta%  Move Log
Cpy%Sync Convert
var  vg0  -wi-ao---- 32.00g
```

We then take the snapshot:

```
$ lvcreate --size 2G --snapshot --name var-snap vg0/var
  Logical volume "var-snap" created
```

Then, we checksum the manifest:

```
$ find /var -type f -exec md5sum {} \; > /root/var-checksum-before.md5
```

We then check for filesystem consistency before the shrink:

```
$ e2fsck -f /dev/vg0/var
e2fsck 1.46.5 (30-Dec-2021)
/dev/vg0/var: clean, 183124/2097152 files, 510293/8388608 blocks
```

Shrinking Filesystem

Always shrink the filesystem to the new desired size before reducing the LV. Here, we aim for 6 GB with headroom above current use:

```
$ resize2fs /dev/vg0/var 6G
resize2fs 1.46.5 (30-Dec-2021)
Resizing the filesystem on /dev/vg0/var to 1572864 (4k)
blocks.
The filesystem on /dev/vg0/var is now 1572864 (4k) blocks
long.
```

If you try to shrink the LV before the filesystem, data loss is likely, always check for a successful resize before proceeding.

Shrinking Logical Volume

Once the filesystem is safely reduced, we then resize the LV itself:

```
$ lvreduce -L 6G /dev/vg0/var
Do you really want to reduce vg0/var? [y/n]: y
  Size of logical volume vg0/var changed from 32.00 GiB to
6.00 GiB.
  Logical volume vg0/var successfully resized.
```

Runing Filesystem Check and Mount

After the reduction, we then check the filesystem again for errors:

```
$ e2fsck -f /dev/vg0/var
e2fsck 1.46.5 (30-Dec-2021)
/dev/vg0/var: clean, 183124/524288 files, 375123/1572864
blocks
```

After this, we then remount and confirm size and usability:

```
$ mount /var
$ df -h /var
```

```
Filesystem             Size  Used Avail Use% Mounted on
/dev/mapper/vg0-var  6.0G  2.6G  3.1G  47% /var
```

Next, we have to compare the new state to the original checksum manifest:

```
$ find /var -type f -exec md5sum {} \; > /root/var-checksum-after.md5
$ diff /root/var-checksum-before.md5 /root/var-checksum-after.md5
# (No output: files match, all data is intact)
```

If at any point the filesystem shows errors, a file is missing, or checksums differ, we have to immediately revert using the snapshot:

```
$ umount /var
$ lvconvert --merge /dev/vg0/var-snap
# Reboot to activate the restored LV state
$ reboot
```

Following is a sample reporting:

```
Snapshot: /dev/vg0/var-snap, 2G
LV before: 32G, after: 6G
Checksum: all files matched before and after shrink
Filesystem: e2fsck clean after resize, no errors
```

Overall, the process of shrinking a logical volume can be safe and fast, only if the right order is followed as we demonstrated in the above.

Rebuilding Degraded RAID

Now somewhere, in the middle of a reporting week, the VM-2's **/data** storage array shows the dreaded "degraded" flag in monitoring. A notification lands suddenly, saying that the one physical disk in the RAID 1 mirror has failed. Although, the application is still running, and no user data has been lost, but the risk is still high, because if another disk fails before we act, the recovery could become impossible.

So here, the priority now is to identify which disk failed, safely replace it with a new member, watch the rebuild progress, and confirm that the RAID is fully healthy before removing any "at risk" status.

Identifying Failed RAID Member

We begin with the RAID status, using **mdadm** for software RAID:

```
$ cat /proc/mdstat
Personalities : [raid1]
md0 : active raid1 sdb1[0] sdc1[1](F)
      52428736 blocks super 1.2 [2/1] [U_]
unused devices: <none>
```

This gives us the output that shows **md0** is a two-disk RAID 1, but only one member (**sdb1[0]**) is active. The **[U_]** means "Up, Down," so the array is degraded. The failed member is **sdc1[1](F)**.

Now to check which physical device this is, we simply run:

```
$ mdadm --detail /dev/md0
/dev/md0:
           Version : 1.2
     Creation Time : ...
        Raid Level : raid1
        Array Size : 52428736 (50.00 GiB 53.69 GB)
     Used Dev Size : 52428736 (50.00 GiB 53.69 GB)
      Raid Devices : 2
     Total Devices : 2
       Persistence : Superblock is persistent
       State : clean, degraded
Active Devices : 1
Working Devices : 1
Failed Devices : 1
 Spare Devices : 0
         Name : ...
```

```
      UUID : ...
    Events : 34
 Number   Major   Minor   RaidDevice State
    0       8       17        0      active sync   /dev/sdb1
    1       8       33        1      faulty   /dev/sdc1
```

Replacing Failed Disk

After identifying the **/dev/sdc1** as failed, power down and physically replace the bad disk, or, in a virtual environment, detach and attach a new blank disk. After the new disk is visible (for example, as **/dev/sdc**), we then create a partition matching the original RAID member type:

```
$ fdisk /dev/sdc
# (create partition 1, type 'fd' for Linux RAID)
```

We then check the partition table:

```
$ lsblk
NAME    MAJ:MIN RM  SIZE RO TYPE MOUNTPOINT
sdb       8:16   0   50G  0 disk
    sdb1     8:17   0   50G  0 part
sdc       8:32   0   50G  0 disk
    sdc1     8:33   0   50G  0 part
```

Adding New Member to Array

We then tell **mdadm** to add the new partition:

```
$ mdadm --add /dev/md0 /dev/sdc1
mdadm: added /dev/sdc1
```

We can also monitor the rebuild:

```
$ watch cat /proc/mdstat
```

The following is a desired output:

```
md0 : active raid1 sdb1[0] sdc1[1]
```

```
      52428736 blocks super 1.2 [2/1] [U_]

      [>....................]  recovery =  1.0%
(524288/52428736) finish=19.3min speed=45360K/sec
```

When the process completes, the array then shows as fully healthy:

```
md0 : active raid1 sdb1[0] sdc1[1]

      52428736 blocks super 1.2 [2/2] [UU]
```

Validating Array State

Always finish with a thorough check of array health:

```
$ mdadm --detail /dev/md0

/dev/md0:

           State : clean

    Active Devices : 2

   Working Devices : 2

   Failed Devices : 0

   Spare Devices : 0

   Number   Major   Minor   RaidDevice State

      0       8       17        0      active sync   /dev/sdb1

      1       8       33        1      active sync   /dev/sdc1
```

We then confirm that the data is readable and no errors appear in logs. Overall, by identifying the failed member, cleanly replacing it, carefully adding it to the array, and watching the rebuild to completion, we can bring systems back to full health with no risk of data loss.

Future-Proofing Mounts

After a routine storage expansion, the VM-2 suddenly began booting with **/data** mounted as read-only, and sometimes failed to mount **/backup** at all. A quick check showed that device names like **/dev/sdb1** had changed after the addition of a new disk. What used to be **/dev/sdb1** was now **/dev/sdc1**, breaking the static device paths in **/etc/fstab**. With every reboot, Linux assigned device names dynamically, depending on disk enumeration order. The result is unpredictable mounts, unbootable nodes, or silent data corruption as filesystems landed in the wrong place. To prevent this class of failure for good, the team decided to migrate all mounts from legacy device paths to stable identifiers, UUIDs and LABELs, so every filesystem always lands on the right target, regardless of hardware shuffles or future storage changes.

We know that the traditional device paths like **/dev/sdb1** are fragile because the kernel assigns them based on probe order, which can change after hardware adds, BIOS updates, or VM migrations. The UUID (Universally Unique Identifier) and LABEL provide persistent, filesystem-level identifiers that never change unless the volume is recreated or explicitly relabeled. So, if we migrate to these identifiers in **/etc/fstab**, the systems become resilient to storage changes, and every mount operation stays consistent across reboots and upgrades.

Identifying Device Paths

To begin with, we first review the existing mounts and locate any device path usage in **/etc/fstab**:

```
$ cat /etc/fstab
/dev/sdb1   /data     ext4   defaults   0 2
/dev/sdc1   /backup   ext4   defaults   0 2
```

We then get the UUID and LABEL for each partition:

```
$ blkid
/dev/sdb1: UUID="3d2456af-1f2c-42f2-8cf4-573d373f9e2c"
TYPE="ext4" LABEL="DATA"
/dev/sdc1: UUID="b8ef34cd-2266-4b95-bd7e-3ad80ab68b24"
TYPE="ext4" LABEL="BACKUP"
```

Using UUID and LABEL

After this we then edit the **/etc/fstab** to reference these identifiers instead of device paths. Using UUID:

```
UUID=3d2456af-1f2c-42f2-8cf4-573d373f9e2c   /data    ext4
defaults   0 2
UUID=b8ef34cd-2266-4b95-bd7e-3ad80ab68b24   /backup ext4
defaults   0 2
```

And, now using the LABEL:

```
LABEL=DATA    /data    ext4   defaults   0 2
```

```
LABEL=BACKUP  /backup  ext4  defaults  0 2
```

We then save the file. The mount syntax stays the same; only the first field changes.

Setting Labels

If a filesystem does not already have a label, add one using **e2label** (for ext4) or the relevant tool for the filesystem:

```
$ e2label /dev/sdb1 DATA
$ e2label /dev/sdc1 BACKUP
```

We then re-check with **blkid** to confirm:

```
$ blkid | grep LABEL
/dev/sdb1: UUID="3d2456af-1f2c-42f2-8cf4-573d373f9e2c"
TYPE="ext4" LABEL="DATA"
/dev/sdc1: UUID="b8ef34cd-2266-4b95-bd7e-3ad80ab68b24"
TYPE="ext4" LABEL="BACKUP"
```

Validating Mounts

We then have to test the new configuration before rebooting, so as to ensure the system will mount correctly:

```
$ sudo umount /data /backup
$ sudo mount -a
```

After this, we then check the mount points:

```
$ findmnt | grep -E '/data|/backup'
/data   /dev/sdb1  ext4  rw,relatime
/backup /dev/sdc1  ext4  rw,relatime
```

The mount sources should show the correct devices, but **/etc/fstab** now refers to them by stable ID.

Confirming Stability

After validation, reboot the system to simulate real-world conditions:

```
$ sudo reboot
```

After this, when the node returns, confirm that all filesystems are mounted as expected and that no mount errors appear:

```
$ findmnt | grep -E '/data|/backup'
/data    /dev/sdb1  ext4  rw,relatime
/backup /dev/sdc1  ext4  rw,relatime
$ journalctl -b -p err --no-pager | grep mount
# (No errors should be listed)
```

If the devices are reassigned, Linux will still mount the right volume in the right place due to UUID/LABEL.

Following is a sample summary for your easy understanding:

```
Old fstab:
/dev/sdb1  /data    ext4  defaults  0 2
New fstab:
UUID=3d2456af-1f2c-42f2-8cf4-573d373f9e2c  /data   ext4
defaults  0 2
Validation:
$ mount -a
$ findmnt | grep /data
/data /dev/sdb1 ext4 rw,relatime
$ sudo reboot
$ findmnt | grep /data
/data /dev/sdc1 ext4 rw,relatime
```

The device paths are highly fragile, but UUID and LABEL are resilient. By migrating **fstab** to stable identifiers and validating mounts before and after a reboot, wecan successfully future-proof systems against disk shuffles, expansions, or migrations, and we will be very sure that every filesystem always lands in the right place, regardless of hardware change.

Knowledge Exercise

1. After editing **/etc/fstab** to add a new mount for **/var**, a system fails to boot and drops into emergency mode with the error:

```
mount: special device UUID=0f9c7e9b-xxxx does not exist
```

Which command will help us quickly verify all available filesystems and their identifiers to fix the issue?

   A. **lsblk -o NAME,SIZE,FSTYPE,UUID**
   B. **du -sh /var**
   C. **uptime**

2. What is the safest order to shrink an oversized logical volume and its filesystem?

   A. Unmount, check filesystem, shrink filesystem, shrink LV, check filesystem again, remount
   B. Shrink LV, then filesystem
   C. Shrink filesystem, then LV, then unmount

3. Before shrinking a logical volume, which method creates an instant rollback point if the process goes wrong?

   A. **lvcreate --size 2G --snapshot --name pre-shrink vg0/var**
   B. **rsync -a /var /tmp/backup**
   C. **mkfs.ext4 /dev/vg0/var**

4. After extending a live filesystem and running **resize2fs**, which command best verifies both the block device size and the available space on the mount?

A.

```
lsblk | grep var
df -h /var
```

B.

```
fdisk -l
free -h
```

C.

```
ps aux | grep var
```

5. When rebuilding a degraded RAID 1 array, which tool provides real-time progress and status of the rebuild?

   A. **cat /proc/mdstat**

B. **dmesg**
C. **fdisk -l**

6. Which of the following **/etc/fstab** entries best prevents mounting errors caused by device renaming after hardware changes?

   A.

```
UUID=6a2c... /data ext4 defaults 0 2
```

   B.

```
/dev/sdb1 /data ext4 defaults 0 2
```

   C.

```
/dev/disk/by-path/pci-0000:00:1f.2-scsi-0:2:0:0-part1 /data
ext4 defaults 0 2
```

7. We want to apply a new label "ARCHIVE" to **/dev/sdd1** and use it in **/etc/fstab**. Which commands should you run?

   A.

```
e2label /dev/sdd1 ARCHIVE
LABEL=ARCHIVE /mnt/archive ext4 defaults 0 2
```

   B.

```
tune2fs -L ARCHIVE /dev/sdd1
LABEL=ARCHIVE /mnt/archive ext4 defaults 0 2
```

   C. Both A and B are valid for ext4 filesystems

8. What is the key advantage of using **LABEL** or **UUID** for mount entries in **/etc/fstab**?

   A. They are persistent and independent of device naming
   B. They always provide higher read speed
   C. They require fewer disk partitions

9. After adding a new disk, the **/data** partition is not mounting on reboot, even though **/etc/fstab** is configured correctly. Which command most reliably tests the new fstab entries before reboot?

   A. **mount -a**
   B. **mkfs.ext4 /dev/sdb1**

C. **ls /data**

10. Which sequence best checks for data integrity after shrinking a filesystem and before deleting the pre-shrink snapshot?

A.

```
find /var -type f -exec md5sum {} \; > /root/after.md5
diff /root/before.md5 /root/after.md5
```

B.

```
rsync -a /var /tmp/backup
rm -rf /tmp/backup
```

C.

```
ls /var
lsblk
```

Note: In this chapter quiz, option A is the correct answer for every question.

CHAPTER 3: USERS, GROUPS, PERMISSIONS AND PAM

Quick User Onboarding

In one of the Mondays and that too early morning, the HR team delivers a spreadsheet listing several new hires who must be granted access to the finance portal infrastructure before business hours. The list includes new analysts, a couple of application developers, and an external auditor who will join only for a quarterly review. Each role requires a specific group assignment. The analysts are to be members of the **analysts** group, developers need access to **devteam**, and the auditor should have only the minimum necessary permissions. And, the compliance expects that every account will have a non-expiring status, a default shell set to **/bin/bash**, and that an audit summary will show each user's group, password status, and the last password change date.

In past quarters, manual onboarding resulted in mistakes, with users receiving the wrong shell, being assigned to the wrong group, or having expiry set incorrectly. This time, the requirement is to automate the process, to batch-create accounts, enforce group and shell policy, and produce an audit record for compliance. So here, the right approach starts with group setup, then uses batch tools for account creation, and finishes with a script-driven audit that gives the compliance team all the evidence they need without extra requests.

Group Creation and Policy Preparation

Here, at first, we start to define the required groups. If the group does not exist, we create it first. Each group reflects a policy tier or a job function.

```
$ sudo groupadd analysts
$ sudo groupadd devteam
$ sudo groupadd auditors
```

Now for each account, we must plan the following requirements:

- Set the shell to **/bin/bash**
- Ensure the account does not expire
- Assign to the correct primary group

Preparing Batch User List

Next, we can expect the HR to sent a file like this:

```
username,role
ananya,analyst
rohit,analyst
jane,analyst
```

```
paul,dev
devi,dev
amira,dev
lucas,auditor
```

We have to convert or save this as **users.csv** for the onboarding script.

Automating Batch User and Group Creation

We will write a small script which can read the user list and apply policy controls as it adds each account. The script reads the CSV, assigns the correct group, and sets up all policy attributes in one sweep.

```
#!/bin/bash
while IFS=, read -r username role
do
  # Map roles to groups
  case $role in
    analyst)
      group="analysts"
      ;;
    dev)
      group="devteam"
      ;;
    auditor)
      group="auditors"
      ;;
    *)
      group="users"
      ;;
  esac
  # Create user, assign primary group, set shell
  sudo useradd -m -g "$group" -s /bin/bash "$username"
```

```
  # Set password to never expire
  sudo chage -M 99999 "$username"
done < users.csv
```

Following is a sample terminal output as accounts are created:

```
$ id ananya
uid=1010(ananya) gid=1013(analysts) groups=1013(analysts)
$ getent passwd paul
paul:x:1012:1014::/home/paul:/bin/bash
$ chage -l lucas
Last password change                                    : Jul
19, 2025
Password expires                                        :
never
Account expires                                         :
never
```

Generating Attribute Audit

After the accounts are created, produce a clear audit record. This report shows username, primary group, supplementary groups, password status, and last password change. It can be saved as a CSV for compliance or internal audit.

```
#!/bin/bash
echo
"username,primary_group,groups,password_status,last_pw_change"
> user_audit.csv
for user in ananya rohit jane paul devi amira lucas
do
  primary_group=$(id -gn "$user")
  all_groups=$(id -Gn "$user" | tr ' ' ':')
  pw_status=$(passwd -S "$user" | awk '{print $2}')
  last_change=$(chage -l "$user" | grep "Last password change"
| cut -d: -f2- | xargs)
```

```
  echo
"$user,$primary_group,$all_groups,$pw_status,$last_change" >>
user_audit.csv
done
```

Given below is the example of a resulting CSV audit file:

```
username,primary_group,groups,password_status,last_pw_change
ananya,analysts,ananya:analysts,P,Jul 19, 2025
rohit,analysts,rohit:analysts,P,Jul 19, 2025
jane,analysts,jane:analysts,P,Jul 19, 2025
paul,devteam,paul:devteam,P,Jul 19, 2025
devi,devteam,devi:devteam,P,Jul 19, 2025
amira,devteam,amira:devteam,P,Jul 19, 2025
lucas,auditors,lucas:auditors,P,Jul 19, 2025
```

In the above, the **P** in password status indicates an active, unlocked password.

Spot Checking

After creation, we then verify any account quickly:

```
$ id jane
uid=1011(jane) gid=1013(analysts) groups=1013(analysts)
$ getent passwd amira
amira:x:1015:1014::/home/amira:/bin/bash
$ chage -l rohit
Last password change                                 : Jul
19, 2025
Password expires                                     :
never
```

This entire workflow ensures that every user receives the correct shell, non-expiry, and group membership with a single, repeatable process.

Fixing Access Failures

Suddenly, the auditor logs in but gets blocked from **/finance/reports**, while the analysts can't read certain logs in **/var/app-logs** either. It turns out that a batch of permissions were changed during the last migration, leaving both teams unable to do their work. We need to get this fixed right away, but with a style that's precise and human, not just "flip a bit and hope."

Getting Access Back

So, our first move is to bring everyone back to their right group. If **/finance/reports** is supposed to be writable by **analysts** and locked away from everyone else, we want to set the group and permissions like this:

```
sudo chown :analysts /finance/reports
sudo chmod 2770 /finance/reports
```

That **2** at the start of **2770** flips on the setgid bit, which basically means every new file or directory inherits the **analysts** group. Now both owner and group get full access, and everyone else stays out.

If we want an auditor to just read a specific file, try this one:

```
sudo chown root:auditors /finance/reports/audit-summary.pdf
sudo chmod 640 /finance/reports/audit-summary.pdf
```

And, if those log files in **/var/app-logs** should be readable for analysts, but only writable by the app, this does the trick as shown below:

```
sudo chown root:analysts /var/app-logs/*
sudo chmod 640 /var/app-logs/*
```

We can also get there with symbolic modes too, like so:

```
chmod g+rX /finance/reports
chmod o-rwx /finance/reports
```

This way, we are handing out exactly the access we want, no more, no less.

Layering on Special Bits

Now, we may need to have new files inside a shared directory to always get the group set. So here, the setgid bit makes it automatic, so no one must remember later:

```
sudo chmod g+s /finance/reports
```

If there's a scratch area like **/shared/tmp** and we don't want users deleting each other's files, the sticky bit is what we are after:

```
sudo chmod +t /shared/tmp
```

Fine-Tuned Controlling

Sometimes the group or owner just isn't enough, especially if we want to grant one-off access. ACLs let us get super precise. To let **lucas** (basically our auditor) read a directory even if he's not in the right group, we must run the following:

```
sudo setfacl -m u:lucas:r /finance/reports
```

To open up the directory for the whole **auditors** group to list and read:

```
sudo setfacl -m g:auditors:rx /finance/reports
```

Now here, if we want to see who gets what to see, then try the following command:

```
getfacl /finance/reports
```

This will let we see exactly who gets what.

Testing as Actual User

This bit's really important. Just because the permissions are set right, doesn't mean they're set correctly. I'd recommend we switch to the user's perspective for a sec and check things from their point of view.

Below is how we do it:

```
sudo -u lucas cat /finance/reports/audit-summary.pdf
sudo -u jane ls /finance/reports
sudo -u rohit tail /var/app-logs/app.log
```

When we run these, we are walking in their shoes. If we see the expected results, file contents, directory listings, log output, then we know the permissions chain is actually working, not just looking right on paper. In the above, it gives us a successful command confirmation about the enforcement of the permission chains. And, it also confirms the restoration of access just as we wanted.

However, if by any chance the operation fails, we can easily review by **ls -l** and **getfacl** and quickly make a fix to it.

Granting Just-Enough Admin

Sometimes, we want to give a developer, operator, or external engineer just enough access to run specific commands, like restarting a service or checking logs, but not the run of the whole system. However, if we let someone use **sudo su -** or give them blanket access, it turns out be highly risky.

So here, what we want is tight, targeted sudo rules, such that the folks get just what they need, and nothing they don't.

Setting up Argument Restrictions

Let us assume that **devi** is joining the on-call rotation. And, she needs to restart the billing API service and view the system journal for it, but shouldn't be able to mess with anything else.

So here, we drop into the sudoers editor safely using visudo:

```
sudo visudo
```

We then scroll down (or use **sudo visudo -f /etc/sudoers.d/devi** for a dedicated file) and add:

```
devi ALL=(root) NOPASSWD: /bin/systemctl restart billing-
api.service, /bin/journalctl -u billing-api.service
```

In the above, following is what's happening:

- **devi** can run **systemctl restart billing-api.service** as root, but not, say, **systemctl stop sshd.service**.
- **devi** can check logs for just the billing API with journalctl.
- The **NOPASSWD:** bit means no password is prompted. If we want a password, just remove it.

This rule makes it so even if she tries something wild, like **sudo rm -rf /**, it will be denied unless it matches those exact commands.

Testing in Second Session

We open a second terminal or SSH session, and either **su** or **SSH** as **devi**. We then put those rules to the test:

```
sudo systemctl restart billing-api.service
```

This should work and not ask for a password (if we included **NOPASSWD**).

We also try something that is outside the rules:

```
sudo systemctl restart sshd.service
```

Here, we will expect a "not allowed" error.

We can also check the logs:

```
sudo journalctl -u billing-api.service | tail -20
```

By this, we get access.

Sudo Rules with Argument Patterns

We can get fancy here wherein we try to allow argument patterns. For example, if we want **paul** to be able to restart any systemd service starting with **app-**:

```
paul ALL=(root) NOPASSWD: /bin/systemctl restart app-*.service
```

This lets **sudo systemctl restart app-logger.service** and **sudo systemctl restart app-auth.service** work, but not unrelated services.

With targeted sudo rules, we can hand out just the right amount of admin power. It keeps the systems safer, the compliance team happier, and makes it crystal clear who can do what.

Restoring Logins after PAM Misstep

Somewhere in the middle of the workl, there was a tweak to **/etc/pam.d/sshd**, which was meant to improve password strength, but instead, everyone's locked out, even the admin's SSH session fails. Only the console or a rescue boot still gives access. So now, the team needs a safe way to restore login, fix the misordered module, and be able to roll back if a future change goes sideways again.

Staging PAM Edits

To begin with, first things first, we must work only from the root console or a second SSH session that stays open. So we never lose the lifeline. Before touching anything, we also save a backup of the PAM config we are about to change:

```
cp /etc/pam.d/sshd /etc/pam.d/sshd.bak-$(date +%Y%m%d%H%M%S)
```

This little move saves the bacon if things get weird.

Correcting Module Order

Next, we then open the problem file, and scan for obvious issues, like:

- Are the "auth" lines in the right order?
- Did we maybe place a **`required`** module after a **`requisite`** one, so that it always blocks?
- Is there a typo in a module name, like **`pam_pwquality.so`** spelled wrong?

Suppose the offending file looks like this:

```
auth requisite pam_deny.so
auth required pam_unix.so
auth required pam_pwquality.so retry=3
```

This order would block every login! The **`pam_deny.so`** line must come last, or it always stops the chain.

We then rearrange as below:

```
auth required pam_unix.so
auth required pam_pwquality.so retry=3
auth requisite pam_deny.so
```

Or, even better, make sure **`pam_deny.so`** is only called as a final catch-all.

Rolling Back

If the test session cannot log in after a change, we can quickly restore the backup. From the root console:

```
cp /etc/pam.d/sshd.bak-* /etc/pam.d/sshd
```

Or, if we get locked out, we then boot into single-user or rescue mode.

Testing Login from Second Session

We have to keep the current SSH or console window open. So for this, in another terminal, you type:

```
ssh localhost
```

or

```
ssh youruser@server
```

If we log in without trouble, we are safe. If not, don't close the original root session. Just go back, fix or revert, and then try again.

This way, if another team member hits a login failure, they see the fix right away and the steps to recover, no need to panic or poke at configs in the dark.

End-to-end Account Hygiene

As time goes by, Linux systems tend to collect old user accounts, passwords that haven't changed in years, and files in sensitive places that end up getting misplaced. If an account isn't being used, it can be an easy way for attackers to get in. It's not good to have a weak password, and if a file has the wrong owner it could leak information or break applications. When you take care of account hygiene in one go, you get rid of risks and keep compliance teams happy, and you don't have to deal with last-minute fire drills.

Rotating Credentials

The first step is to refresh credentials so that active users stay protected. We can rotate passwords for users in bulk using a simple script or manual loop. In the below, we will do it for several team members:

```
for user in jane rohit dev paul; do
  sudo passwd "$user"
done
```

Each command in the above prompts for a new password. If we use SSH keys, rotate those too by updating the user's **~/.ssh/authorized_keys**.

So now, to check when a password was last changed:

```
chage -l jane
```

In it, look for a recent date under "Last password change." This helps us spot accounts overdue for a reset.

Expiring Stale Accounts

The accounts that have not been used for a long time, or belong to people who have left the team, should be locked or set to expire. To see who hasn't logged in recently, we can try:

```
lastlog | grep -v "Never"
```

For accounts we want to expire immediately (preventing new logins):

```
sudo usermod --expiredate 1 lucas
```

Or, to lock the account without deleting it:

```
sudo passwd -l dev
```

If we want to list all locked accounts, run:

```
sudo passwd -S -a | grep ' L '
```

And for a quick cleanup, we can loop through a list and expire them:

```
for user in olduser1 olduser2; do
  sudo usermod --expiredate 1 "$user"
done
```

Validating Ownership

The files in critical directories, like **/var/app-logs**, **/finance/reports**, or **/srv/securedata**, need to be owned by the right users or groups. To spot files that drifted into the wrong hands, we can use:

```
find /finance/reports ! -user root ! -group analysts
```

This lists files not owned by root or not in the analysts group.

Now, to fix ownership in one pass:

```
sudo chown -R root:analysts /finance/reports
```

It's a good move to do this after every major round of onboarding or offboarding. We can also check permissions for anything world-writable (which usually isn't safe):

```
find /srv/securedata -perm -o+w
```

If we spot any, consider tightening with:

```
chmod o-w filename
```

That's how a full account hygiene pass looks, rotate what's active, lock what's stale, and make sure sensitive files are in the right hands.

Knowledge Exercise

1. Which command would create a new user **linda**, assign the primary group **auditors**, set the default shell to **/bin/bash**, and ensure a home directory is created?

   A. **useradd -m -g auditors -s /bin/bash linda**

   B. **adduser linda auditors /bin/bash**

   C. **useradd auditors linda /bin/bash**

2. We receive a request to quickly onboard six new analysts, all with the same shell and group. Which script section achieves this for names in a file called **analysts.txt**?

   A.

```
while read name; do
useradd -m -g analysts -s /bin/bash "$name"
done < analysts.txt
```

B.

```
for name in analysts.txt; do
useradd "$name"
done
```

C.

```
cat analysts.txt | useradd -g analysts
```

3. After onboarding, we want to prove all users' password expiry is set to "never." Which command gives us that audit in one pass?

   A. **chage -l username**

   B. **passwd -x 0 username**

   C. **usermod -e 0 username**

4. A developer complains of "permission denied" when writing to **/var/app-logs/log.txt**, even though their group should have write access. Which command helps us check the group ownership and permissions in detail?

   A. **ls -l /var/app-logs/log.txt**

   B. **groups log.txt**

   C. **ps aux | grep app-logs**

5. What does the command **chmod 2770 /finance/reports** accomplish for a team folder?

   A. Sets setgid so new files inherit group, full access for owner/group, none for others

   B. Sets sticky bit for file retention

   C. Removes all permissions except for owner

6. We want to grant **lucas** read access to **/finance/reports** but he's not in the right group. Which command achieves this using ACLs?

   A. **setfacl -m u:lucas:r /finance/reports**

   B. **chmod u+r /finance/reports**

   C. **chown lucas /finance/reports**

7. Which **sudoers** entry would let user **devi** restart the **billing-api.service** without a password, but block all other **systemctl** usage?

A.

```
devi ALL=(root) NOPASSWD: /bin/systemctl restart billing-
api.service
```

B.

```
devi ALL=(root) NOPASSWD: /bin/systemctl *
```

C.

```
devi ALL=(root) NOPASSWD: ALL
```

8. If an incorrect change to **/etc/pam.d/sshd** causes all logins to fail, what is the safest way to recover?

   A. Restore the last backup from console or rescue mode

   B. Try to log in again repeatedly

C. Reboot and hope for the best

9. Which command locks the user **olga**'s account immediately, preventing further logins but keeping her files?

   A. **passwd -l olga**

   B. **userdel olga**

   C. **chsh -s /sbin/nologin olga**

10. We want to quickly find any files under **/srv/securedata** not owned by **root** or group **secure**. Which command gives us this result?

    A. **find /srv/securedata ! -user root ! -group secure**

    B. **ls -l /srv/securedata**

    C. **getfacl /srv/securedata**

Note: In this chapter quiz, option A is the correct answer for every question.

CHAPTER 4: PACKAGES, REPOSITORIES AND SCHEDULING

Almost every Linux system, whether it is running in the cloud, a datacenter, or a laptop in a café, survives on a steady diet of software packages. These packages bring security updates, new features, and bug fixes, all managed by a complex ecosystem of repositories, mirrors, and local caches. When everything works, we barely notice, the right package appears, installs without fuss, and updates roll out automatically.

But when things go wrong, a single broken repository or a corrupted metadata cache can halt productivity for an entire team. Suddenly, installs fail, dependencies cannot be resolved, and even the tried-and-true **`apt update`** turns into a wall of errors. With real-world deadlines and security requirements, waiting for upstream fixes is not an option. This chapter will get us the solutions for restoring package managers, fixing broken repos, speeding up updates, and mastering scheduled jobs, all with evidence we can show the team.

Repairing Broken Repositories

Let us think of a situation that we are in the middle of a routine update when the package manager throws a fit: "repository not found," "failed to fetch," or "signature verification failed." Team members ping us saying even basic installs are failing, and the next build cannot move forward. The repository mirror may have gone offline, the metadata could be stale, or a GPG key may have expired. The team is blocked and needs the repositories working again, fast, without spending hours digging through cryptic logs.

Refreshing Repository Metadata

To begin, start by refreshing the metadata, which is the most lightweight fix by running:

```
sudo apt update
```

If we see errors about "InRelease" or "Release" files missing, the metadata may be stale or corrupted.

Replacing Different Mirrors

Sometimes, a particular mirror goes down or gets outdated. The fastest fix is to swap to a different mirror. So here, we can open **`/etc/apt/sources.list`** or a file under **`/etc/apt/sources.list.d/`** and change the mirror URL. For example, switch from:

```
deb http://archive.ubuntu.com/ubuntu/ focal main restricted
```

to a local or faster mirror:

```
deb http://in.archive.ubuntu.com/ubuntu/ focal main restricted
```

After saving, run:

```
sudo apt update
```

Then refresh the metadata again.

Cleaning Package Caches

The corrupted or partial caches often block installs. So here, we will clear them out. It is quite safe and fast.

```
sudo apt clean
sudo apt update
```

If we still hit issues, then we need to removing the lock files and check for disk space:

```
sudo rm /var/lib/apt/lists/lock
df -h
```

Running Signature Checks

The signatures in repositories stop us from getting dodgy packages, but sometimes GPG keys expire or go missing. When we see errors like "NO_PUBKEY" or "The following signatures couldn't be verified," we need to fetch the right key.

So here, the error message will usually mention the missing key. We can import it with:

```
sudo apt-key adv --keyserver keyserver.ubuntu.com --recv-keys
<KEYID>
```

Once the keys are imported, we can then rerun the update command.

After fixes, we then need to verify the result with:

```
sudo apt update
```

if we get a clean run (no errors about metadata, signatures, or mirrors), then it is the proof of success. For extra confidence, we can also install a small package:

```
sudo apt install cowsay
```

If the install works, it means the repositories are back in action.

Pinning Versions and Rolling Back Regressions

Installing Specific Versions

Sometimes, the newest version just does not work with the app, or a regression sneaks in after a routine upgrade. So here, to avoid surprises, we can install a specific version of a package instead of always grabbing the latest.

At first, we will see the available versions:

```
apt list -a nginx
```

To install a particular one (let's say version 1.18.0):

```
sudo apt install nginx=1.18.0-0ubuntu1
```

This pins the package at the chosen version.

Locking Package Version

Once we have the version we want, we lock it in so upgrades won't sneak it forward.

```
sudo apt-mark hold nginx
```

To check which packages are held:

```
apt-mark showhold
```

If we want to remove the lock when we are ready:

```
sudo apt-mark unhold nginx
```

Downgrading Package

Similarly, when a new version causes problems, we can always roll back to the older one.

```
sudo apt install nginx=1.18.0-0ubuntu1
```

Smoke Testing

We can't just blindly trust that the installation is finished. After we have pinned or rolled back, it's a good idea to run a smoke test. This is a quick check to see if the main functionality works and if there are any immediate side effects.

For a web server like nginx, wee can try:

```
sudo systemctl restart nginx
curl -I http://localhost
```

If we get **HTTP/1.1 200 OK** in the output, it means the nginx is up and answering.

And, if we are working with a library or a CLI tool, we just need to run the main command and check for errors:

```
nginx -t
```

And, we need to look for the line:

```
nginx: configuration file /etc/nginx/nginx.conf test is successful
```

Or, for a database server:

```
sudo systemctl restart postgresql
psql -U postgres -c 'SELECT version();'
```

With this, we are confirming that not only did the package downgrade or pin, but also that nothing broke in the process.

A smoke test is the "early warning system." It is especially handy if:

- We are about to roll this out on more systems,
- We need proof for the team or management that the rollback fixed the symptom, or
- We want to spot hidden breakage before users do

If the test fails, we can immediately try a different version, re-run the rollback, or dig deeper knowing the root cause is probably the new package version, not a random unrelated change.

Upgrading to 'systemd' Timers

Well, it's 2 a.m. and, guess what, the daily backup cron job has failed again, but not in any loud way. There are no logs or alerts, and the team doesn't notice until a restore is needed. It's the same story with routine cleanups and reporting scripts: cron entries can break, collide with each other, or even disappear when a user's crontab is overwritten. It's all about reliability, with built-in logs and the ability to run jobs on-demand or see exactly when they last executed.

Migrating Cron Job

Let's say we have got this old cron job, running as root:

```
0 2 * * * /usr/local/bin/db_backup.sh
```

The goal is to have this same backup job managed as a systemd service and timer, with logging, status checks, and easy manual triggering.

Create 'systemd' Service Unit

So here, we will begin with creating a simple service file **/etc/systemd/system/db-backup.service**:

```
[Unit]
Description=Nightly Database Backup
[Service]
Type=oneshot
ExecStart=/usr/local/bin/db_backup.sh
StandardOutput=journal
StandardError=journal
```

It will confirm to us that every run of the script is logged into the system journal, along with any errors.

Create 'systemd' Timer Unit

Now, we will create the timer file **/etc/systemd/system/db-backup.timer**:

```
[Unit]
Description=Nightly Database Backup Timer
[Timer]
OnCalendar=02:00
Persistent=true
[Install]
WantedBy=timers.target
```

Here, **OnCalendar=02:00** means run at 2 a.m. every day. And, the **Persistent=true** means if the system was off at 2 a.m., it'll catch up on the next boot.

Next, we then enable and start the timer:

```
sudo systemctl daemon-reload
sudo systemctl enable --now db-backup.timer
```

We can see all active timers:

```
systemctl list-timers
```

Running Jobs On-Demand

If we want to trigger the backup job right now, then we simply run:

```
sudo systemctl start db-backup.service
```

Here, we no need to wait until the next scheduled time. It is perfect for our testing or urgent fixes.

Capturing Timestamped Output

Most of the output from the job is automatically logged by systemd. So, in case, if we want to view logs for a specific run:

```
journalctl -u db-backup.service --since "today"
```

or for the latest run:

```
journalctl -u db-backup.service -n 50
```

This will give us the output lines with timestamps and any errors, way more useful than the old cron mail output that often went nowhere.

If we want to save logs to a file every run, we can simply add this to the **[Service]** section:

```
ExecStart=/usr/local/bin/db_backup.sh >>
/var/log/db_backup.log 2>&1
```

Or just rely on **journalctl** for a searchable, timestamped log of every execution.

Troubleshooting

We can check the last time the timer fired, next run time, and status all in one place:

```
systemctl status db-backup.timer
systemctl list-timers | grep db-backup
```

Missed runs (if the server was down) will be listed with **Persistent=true**, so we never miss a backup.

If the job fails, systemd's log will show exactly when and why, along with the exit code.

Moving cron jobs to systemd timers makes every scheduled task more visible, reliable, and easier to audit. We gain on-demand control, automatic catch-up for missed runs, and all the logs we need to prove to the team (or the future self) that the job ran and what the outcome was.

Diffs, Status, And Smoke Testing

Every time we change a config, deploy a package or tweak a unit file, a quick "works for me" doesn't cut it. If we include the what changed (diffs), current service status, and endpoint checks with the deployment, anyone reviewing or troubleshooting later can spot what really happened. This means no guesswork, no finger-pointing, just clear, friendly proof.

Capturing Config Diffs

Before we make a change, maybe to **/etc/nginx/nginx.conf** or a systemd unit, we will grab a diff so we can show exactly what we changed. This is easy with **diff** or **git**:

```
diff -u /etc/nginx/nginx.conf{.bak,}
```

Or, if we keep configs in git, then we just have to run:

```
git diff
```

We then need to save this diff output to a text file or paste it into the change ticket, merge request, or Slack thread.

Recording Service Status

Right after deploying the change, we then will collect the systemd status for the affected service. For example, after updating the nginx config, we will restart and capture the status:

```
sudo systemctl restart nginx
sudo systemctl status nginx
```

After this, we then copy the output that shows:

- Active/running status
- Main PID
- Any warnings or errors
- Timestamps for the last restart

For ongoing proof, we can even include a log snippet:

```
journalctl -u nginx --since "5 min ago"
```

We then paste it in with the diff for a complete "before and after" view.

Capturing Smoke Test Results

As we learned previously, the smoke test is just a simple, fast way to check the key features right after a change. So here, for a web service, we will run:

```
curl -I http://localhost
```

The output should show:

```
HTTP/1.1 200 OK
```

For an API, we might:

```
curl -X GET http://localhost:8000/api/health
```

If we get the expected JSON, or a status code like **200**, we are good.

For a database migration, the smoke test could be as simple as:

```
psql -U appuser -d mydb -c "SELECT COUNT(*) FROM
important_table;"
```

We only need to include the command and output in the deployment notes or PR. That way, anyone reviewing knows the change not only applied cleanly, but the service works right now.

When we wrap a change with these three items, diff, status, and smoke test, we are setting a gold standard for operational hygiene. This makes peer review instant, troubleshooting fast, and audit trails rock-solid. Even if we are just working solo, this habit saves future we a ton of time figuring out "what happened" and "did it actually work?"

Speeding Installs with Smart Caching

The first time we build or install a set of packages on a new VM, everything is downloaded from scratch. That's fine once, but in a busy environment or CI/CD pipeline, waiting for the same packages to come down, over and over, eats up time and bandwidth. The concept of smart caching means we pre-load, store, or "warm up" the most common packages, so installs become nearly instant.

Tuning Local Package Caching

For this, we will first set up a caching proxy like **apt-cacher-ng** so that once any machine fetches a package, others get it instantly from the local network.

```
sudo apt install apt-cacher-ng
```

On all client machines, we will point the APT to the proxy. And, we will add this to **/etc/apt/apt.conf.d/02proxy**:

```
Acquire::http::Proxy "http://your-cache-server:3142";
```

Once we are set, we then run:

```
sudo apt update
sudo apt install build-essential git curl
```

The first fetch comes from the internet, but all repeats are lightning fast via cache. If we know certain packages are always needed, we can always pre-warm the cache:

```
sudo apt install --download-only nginx build-essential python3
```

We can also use local repositories or snapshot mirrors if the environment is large.

Measuring Speedup

It is quite easy. Following is how we turn this from a claim into evidence.

Measure Cold Install

First, we clear the cache and time a real install:

```
sudo apt clean
time sudo apt install -y nginx
```

From the output, we need to note the elapsed real time.

Measure Warm Install

Now, we run it again (no cache cleaning):

```
time sudo apt install -y nginx
```

This time, we will see a dramatic drop in the install time, sometimes from 30+ seconds to under 5.

Graphing or Recording Results

If we want a quick "before and after" for the team or report, we can run both commands and capture their output.

Following is the sample output:

```
First install (cold): real    0m32.114s
Second install (warm): real   0m4.230s
```

This gives us the proof we can point to, not just "it feels faster," but numbers the team or auditors can check.

Checking Cache

On the proxy server (**`apt-cacher-ng`**), we can check the statistics page at:

```
http://your-cache-server:3142/acng-report.html
```

If the cache fills up, we can prune it with:

```
sudo apt-cacher-ng -c /etc/apt-cacher-ng/ -C expire
```

It's all about showing the team real, repeatable wins by warming up the cache and measuring the improvement. We're not just going to say "trust me, it's better now," but actually provide proof that the Linux installs are running at top speed. If you need tips on scaling this to hundreds of servers or integrating with the artifact storage, just let me know!

Knowledge Exercise

1. After running **`sudo apt update`**, we see "Failed to fetch" errors for multiple repositories. What is the fastest first troubleshooting step?

   A. Refresh repository metadata with **`sudo apt update`**

   B. Replace repository mirrors in **`sources.list`**

   C. Clear the package cache with **`sudo apt clean`**

2. Your team needs to install **nginx** version **1.18.0** on all servers, and prevent future upgrades. Which command achieves this?

   A. **sudo apt-mark hold nginx**

   B. **sudo apt-get upgrade nginx**

   C. **sudo apt-cache policy nginx**

3. A critical package was accidentally upgraded, causing regressions. How can we roll back to the previous version?

   A. **sudo dnf downgrade <package>**

   B. **sudo apt remove <package>**

   C. **sudo dnf clean all**

4. After editing **/etc/apt/sources.list**, what command tests if the new mirror is working and fetches fresh metadata?

   A. **sudo apt update**

   B. **sudo apt install**

   C. **sudo apt-key add**

5. What is the most reliable way to confirm if a systemd timer job ran successfully and captured logs?

   A. **journalctl -u <service-name>**

   B. **crontab -l**

   C. **atq**

6. We want to prove a config change actually took place. Which method provides the most direct evidence?

   A. Save the **diff** between the original and changed config

   B. Delete the old config file

   C. Describe changes in an email

7. What's the best quick "smoke test" after rolling back a package version for a web server?

   A. **curl -I http://localhost**

   B. **systemctl list-timers**

   C. **apt-cache policy <webserver>**

8. We want to keep the RPM or DEB files after install so future installs run faster. Which setting or tool helps with this?

A. Set **keepcache=True** in **/etc/dnf/dnf.conf** or use a local caching proxy

B. Set **autoclean=true** in apt config

C. Add **purge-old** to dnf.conf

9. A team member says their scheduled job "never runs," but we have migrated it to a systemd timer. What command quickly proves if and when it last ran?

   A. **systemctl list-timers**

   B. **cronstatus**

   C. **yum makecache**

10. How do we measure and prove that caching made package installs faster?

   A. Run **time sudo apt install <package>** before and after enabling cache, and compare real times

   B. Run **apt update** repeatedly

   C. Use **ls /var/cache/apt/archives**

Note: In this chapter quiz, option A is the correct answer for every question.

Chapter 5: Networking and Name Services

Almost everything on modern Linux systems relies on stable network connections, whether it's updating packages, distributed builds, DNS queries or accessing remote APIs. For most teams, networking is one of those things that just works until it suddenly doesn't. If there's a typo in a static IP configuration or the gateway address is in the wrong place, the server that was working fine on the network becomes unreachable. The phone rings, the monitoring goes red and the clock starts ticking.

In this chapter, we'll go through solutions to get Linux systems back online quickly, like fixing static profiles, dealing with DNS, troubleshooting name resolution, and fixing common connectivity hiccups. These are fixes we can use with confidence, even if we're staring at a server console in the middle of the night.

Recovering Connectivity

When you use static network profiles, you can predict how things will work. This means that a server gets the same IP address, gateway and DNS every time. But a single mistake in **`/etc/network/interfaces`**, **`/etc/netplan/*.yaml`**, or a **`nmcli`** static profile, and the system is instantly cut off. Maybe the subnet mask is wrong, the gateway is unreachable, or we landed outside the switch's allowed VLAN. Sometimes, a misconfigured static profile even conflicts with the DHCP scope, creating IP wars on the network. The system might lose connectivity at boot or after a simple "network reload," leaving we on the console with no ping, no SSH, and no web.

Identifying Fault

So here, we start from the console or out-of-band management, IPMI, iLO, or a virtual console, because remote access is usually gone:

```
ip addr
ip route
```

Here, we are looking for the current IP, subnet, and any default gateway. If we see no IP or the wrong subnet, the static config is likely to blame.

Temporary Fallback to DHCP

For quick access, we bring up the interface with DHCP or a known-good fallback:

```
sudo ip addr flush dev eth0
sudo dhclient eth0
```

or, for a manual address:

```
sudo ip addr add 192.168.1.200/24 dev eth0
sudo ip route add default via 192.168.1.1
```

Next, we then check if we can ping the gateway:

```
ping -c 2 192.168.1.1
```

We then test the internet:

```
ping -c 2 8.8.8.8
```

Correcting Configuration

Next, we then edit the offending config file:

```
sudo nano /etc/netplan/01-netcfg.yaml
```

In this, we make sure the IP address, netmask, gateway, and DNS are all correct. Given below is a safe static config example:

```
network:
  version: 2
  ethernets:
    eth0:
      addresses: [192.168.1.200/24]
      gateway4: 192.168.1.1
      nameservers:
        addresses: [8.8.8.8, 8.8.4.4]
```

For **/etc/network/interfaces**:

```
auto eth0
iface eth0 inet static
    address 192.168.1.200
    netmask 255.255.255.0
    gateway 192.168.1.1
```

```
    dns-nameservers 8.8.8.8 8.8.4.4
```

And, for **nmcli/NetworkManager**:

```
nmcli con edit "System eth0"
set ipv4.addresses 192.168.1.200/24
set ipv4.gateway 192.168.1.1
set ipv4.dns 8.8.8.8,8.8.4.4
set ipv4.method manual
save
quit
nmcli con up "System eth0"
```

After saving the changes:

```
sudo netplan apply
```

And, with /etc/network/interfaces:

```
sudo systemctl restart networking
nmcli con up "System eth0"
```

We then test again:

```
ip addr show eth0
ip route
ping -c 2 8.8.8.8
ping -c 2 google.com
```

If everything checks out, SSH or web access should return instantly.

That's how we bring a server back from a broken static profile, using a fallback, correcting the settings, and verifying step by step so the fix is proven, not just guessed.

Fixing Asymmetric Routing

Some or the other day, we are going to work on a server with two NICs: **`eth0`** is connected to the production subnet, and **`eth1`** is used for internal backups or a private management network.

Now here, after setting up a static route or a secondary gateway, connections from certain remote hosts either hang or get dropped. The logins might succeed from one subnet but fail from another, or we notice some requests arrive but never return. The core of the problem is asymmetric routing, where incoming traffic takes one interface, but the reply leaves out the other, often getting blocked by upstream firewalls or failing TCP checks.

Reading Routes and Rules

At first, we get our bearings. We start by dumping the full routing table and any policy rules:

```
ip route show
ip rule show
```

We might see something like this:

```
default via 192.168.1.1 dev eth0
192.168.10.0/24 dev eth1 proto kernel scope link src
192.168.10.5
```

Or policy rules such as:

```
0:      from all lookup local
32766:  from all lookup main
32767:  from all lookup default
```

Here, we want to confirm which subnet gets which gateway, and whether return traffic will "stick" to the same interface.

Adjusting Metrics

When both interfaces claim a default route, the Linux picks the one with the lowest metric. If the static routes have equal metrics, outgoing packets might leave the wrong way. To fix this, we set explicit metrics.

For example, to prefer **eth0** for default internet access and keep **eth1** just for its subnet:

```
sudo ip route add default via 192.168.1.1 dev eth0 metric 100
sudo ip route add default via 192.168.10.1 dev eth1 metric 200
```

Here, we can also add policy rules so that any traffic sourced from **192.168.10.5** always uses the correct table and gateway:

```
sudo ip rule add from 192.168.10.5/32 table 101
sudo ip route add default via 192.168.10.1 dev eth1 table 101
```

Now, any reply to connections that entered via **eth1** will go back out the same way. For more persistent changes, we can add these entries to the network config files.

Validating Return Paths using Counters

After making the changes, we want real evidence that routes are symmetric. For this, we will monitor the interface counters before and after a test:

```
ip -s link show eth0
ip -s link show eth1
```

Next, we watch **RX** (receive) and **TX** (transmit) counters as we ping or curl from different networks.

```
ping 192.168.10.5
ssh user@192.168.10.5
```

We also watch which interface's RX/TX increases.

```
sudo tcpdump -i eth0 host <test-remote-ip>
sudo tcpdump -i eth1 host <test-remote-ip>
```

After this, we start a connection, and confirm both request and reply travel the same interface. If we see replies exiting a different interface than the request arrived on, revisit the route and rule metrics.

This whole thing not only proves the fix, but also gives us a blueprint to solve future asymmetric routing surprises quickly.

Restoring Service Reachability

Somewhere in the middle of the busy day, the support team pings. They say that the monitoring probe or a client system suddenly cannot connect to the web or SSH service. The firewall was "tightened" for security, but now something is broken. The goal here is to identify which rule is blocking, make the narrowest change possible (no risky "accept all"), and prove it works with a quick test from the client.

Reading Firewall Counters

We begin by looking at packet counters. Here, it shows which rules are hit and which ones are dropping packets.

Like, for nftables:

```
sudo nft list ruleset
sudo nft list chain inet filter input
```

So here, to see counters in action, we will focus on lines with "packets" and "bytes" counts. We run this, then try the test connection, and see which rule's count increases.

And, for iptables:

```
sudo iptables -L -n -v
```

This shows us which chain and rule is matching (look for high packet or byte counts, or ones that increase when we try a connection).

For example:

```
Chain INPUT (policy DROP 0 packets, 0 bytes)
 pkts bytes target     prot opt in     out     source
destination
   22  1568 ACCEPT     tcp  --  *      *       0.0.0.0/0
0.0.0.0/0            tcp dpt:22
    0     0 ACCEPT     tcp  --  *      *       192.168.1.50
0.0.0.0/0            tcp dpt:80
```

In the above, if the connection attempt increases the "pkts" counter next to a DROP or no ACCEPT, we know where we are blocked.

Adding Narrowest Allowance

Next, we then want to allow HTTP (port 80) only from a monitoring server at **192.168.1.50**, not the world.

So here, for nftables:

```
sudo nft add rule inet filter input ip saddr 192.168.1.50 tcp
dport 80 accept
```

This rule is precise, just that source IP, just TCP, just port 80.

And, for iptables:

```
sudo iptables -A INPUT -p tcp -s 192.168.1.50 --dport 80 -j
ACCEPT
```

Now here, we must always make sure that we add the rule above any broad DROP or REJECT lines, or before a "deny all" default policy.

Confirming Client Probe

After this, we then move over to the monitoring or client system, and test the connection.

Like, for HTTP:

```
curl -I http://your-server
```

Here, we want to see **`HTTP/1.1 200 OK`** or the app's greeting.

And, for SSH:

```
ssh youruser@your-server
```

If the probe succeeds, we can say that we have made the change as needed, nothing more, nothing less.

This is all that how we restore the right amount of access, like to read the counters, add the narrowest rule, and confirm it works with a real test.

Clearing Port Conflicts and Listening Services

Imagine, we just deployed the shiny new API or web service, but the process fails to start or says "address already in use." Sometimes, everything runs but clients can't connect, maybe the wrong IP is bound, or something else already grabbed the port. So here, getting to the bottom of who owns the port and freeing it up is critical for smooth, dependable connections.

Finding Busy Port Owners

We start by checking which process is holding the port we need. If we expect the service to use port 8080 and it's failing, we will find out who's there already:

```
sudo lsof -i :8080
```

or

```
sudo netstat -tulpn | grep 8080
```

or, on modern systems,

```
sudo ss -ltnp | grep 8080
```

This shows the process name, PID, and user that owns the port.

Following is the sample output:

```
COMMAND   PID  USER   FD   TYPE DEVICE SIZE/OFF NODE NAME
python3 1438  root   12u  IPv4  19326       0t0  TCP *:8080
(LISTEN)
```

With this, we know what's actually using the port.

Adjusting Bindings

If the process isn't needed, we then need to stop or kill it:

```
sudo systemctl stop old-service
sudo kill 1438
```

Or, if it's a zombie or stray process, we need a forceful kill to clear the port:

```
sudo kill -9 1438
```

Sometimes, both services are needed, but only one should use that port. So here, we will change the config for one of them, edit the service file, the application config, or the listening address.

For example, to bind the new app to 0.0.0.0 (all interfaces) or to a specific IP:

```
[Service]
ExecStart=/usr/bin/myapp --bind 0.0.0.0:8080
```

We then restart the service after us make the change.

Proving External Reachability

Once the service is listening, we then check that it's open and reachable, not just locally, but from another machine.

```
ss -ltnp | grep 8080
```

if you want to see **0.0.0.0:8080** or the public IP listed under "Local Address", then from another system:

```
curl -I http://your-server:8080
```

Or else, we may use **nc** (netcat) to test raw connectivity:

```
nc -zv your-server 8080
```

If we get a **Connection refused**, we then check the firewall (use **sudo iptables -L -n -v** or **sudo nft list ruleset**). If we get a timeout, we must make sure the service is bound to the right address, not just **127.0.0.1**.

Knowledge Exercise

1. After setting a static IP in **/etc/netplan/01-netcfg.yaml**, the server loses network access after reboot. Which command should we use first to check if any IP is assigned?

   A. **ip addr**

   B. **nmcli con show**

   C. **route -n**

2. We have two NICs (eth0 and eth1). Traffic from the backup network (eth1) arrives, but replies are sent out eth0, causing connections to fail. What adjustment best solves the asymmetric routing?

   A. Add a policy routing rule and specific route for eth1 traffic

   B. Increase MTU on eth0

   C. Use DHCP on both interfaces

3. After a change to static routing, we want to prove which interfaces handle traffic from a given subnet. What command pair helps most?

   A. **ip -s link show eth0** and **ip -s link show eth1**

   B. **ifup eth0** and **ifdown eth1**

   C. **route add default gw**

4. We suspect the firewall is blocking incoming HTTP (port 80) connections. Which command for nftables lists rules and packet counters for the input chain?

   A. **sudo nft list chain inet filter input**

   B. **nft flush ruleset**

C. **iptables -F**

5. We want to allow SSH from just a single jump box (**192.168.1.10**) using iptables. Which rule is correct?

   A. **iptables -A INPUT -p tcp -s 192.168.1.10 --dport 22 -j ACCEPT**

   B. **iptables -A INPUT -p udp --dport 22 -j ACCEPT**

   C. **iptables -A INPUT --dport 22 -j ACCEPT**

6. Which command confirms if a process is currently listening on port 5432?

   A. **ss -ltnp | grep 5432**

   B. **ping 5432**

   C. **curl localhost:5432**

7. We clear a port conflict and restart the service, but users still can't connect from outside. What's the next best check?

   A. Review the firewall rules and service's listening address

   B. Reboot the server

   C. Delete and reinstall the package

8. When verifying that a firewall change worked, which is the best confirmation method?

   A. Probe the service from a client system and check the firewall rule's packet counter

   B. Look at system logs

   C. List all installed packages

9. On a multihomed server, which tool shows all routing rules by priority?

   A. **ip rule show**

   B. **netstat -rn**

   C. **route**

10. We want to prove a service is reachable on port 8080 from a remote client. Which command should we use from the client?

    A. **curl -I http://server:8080**

    B. **ls -l /proc/net/tcp**

    C. **df -h**

Note: In this chapter quiz, option A is the correct answer for every question.

Chapter 6: Host Security, SELinux or AppArmor and Firewalls

The security of our systems is not something we just switch on or off. From day one, every Linux system needs to be hardened to stay safe. But it's only natural to feel a bit anxious about making changes, especially if a small mistake could stop users or break a service we all need. The best way to approach security is by taking small steps, recording what changes, and keeping every tweak easy to undo. That way, the team can keep locking things down without worrying about unexpected problems or long outages.

In this chapter, we'll go through recipes that'll help you feel totally confident about getting the hosts on board. We'll work out how to save the work before any changes, test that services and logins are working properly, and always have a safety rope ready.

Hardening using Safe Rollbacks

Before making any change to a security setting, like turning off root SSH login or updating a firewall rule, we will ensure that we are saving the current file. For example, we will simply run:

```
sudo cp /etc/ssh/sshd_config /etc/ssh/sshd_config.bak.$(date
+%Y%m%d%H%M%S)
```

If we want to track every update, it's a good idea to start a git repository inside **/etc**. All we need to do is:

```
cd /etc
sudo git init
sudo git add ssh/ firewall/ selinux/ apparmor/
sudo git commit -m "First security snapshot"
```

From here on, each change can be committed, described, and rolled back with one command.

Whenever we need to harden a service, open its config, adjust the setting, and then save or commit the work right away. We just need to restart the service to apply the change, and then log the result.

Validating Authentication and Service Health

After making a change, we need to test that the system is still usable for the right people. For example, after disabling root SSH logins, we can try logging in from another terminal as a regular user:

```
ssh user@host
```

The root account should be blocked, and other users should be able to log in as usual.

We can also check the firewalls, and it is done by simply probing the allowed ports. We can witness the following example:

```
nc -zv host 22 80 443
```

Next, we can watch for open ports to confirm that only the expected services are reachable. For SELinux or AppArmor changes, we can try running the protected app and see if anything is denied. If there is trouble, we can check the logs with:

```
sudo ausearch -m avc
sudo journalctl -xe | grep DENIED
```

So here, each time we finish a test, we take note of what works and what doesn't.

Keeping Rollback Ready

If we run into trouble, we can get back to a safe state. For it, we just restore the backup or check out the previous config from git:

```
sudo cp /etc/ssh/sshd_config.bak.20240718 /etc/ssh/sshd_config
sudo systemctl restart sshd
```

or

```
sudo git checkout HEAD~1 ssh/sshd_config
sudo systemctl restart sshd
```

If the issue was with a firewall or security policy, we can roll those back just as easily. This habit makes it easy to show what we did and why, and helps the team stay bold about hardening. We never have to worry about breaking things, because getting back to safety is always just one step away.

Issuing Keys, CSRs And Certificates

Generating Private Keys

First, let's make a private key for the server or application. For this, we will make use of OpenSSL, and run:

```
openssl genpkey -algorithm RSA -out server.key -pkeyopt
rsa_keygen_bits:2048
```

After this, we will now have a secure **server.key** file. We must keep this file safe, and should never share the private key with anyone.

If we need an EC key instead (for modern TLS):

```
openssl ecparam -genkey -name prime256v1 -out server.key
```

Creating Certificate Signing Request (CSR)

Next, we make a CSR. This is what you'll send to the certificate authority (CA), or sign with the own CA if we are running an internal PKI.

```
openssl req -new -key server.key -out server.csr
```

We will be prompted for details like country, organization, and, most importantly, **Common Name (CN)**. This should match the hostname, such as **myapp.example.com**.

If we need Subject Alternative Names (SANs), we can create a config file like **csr.conf**:

```
[req]
default_bits        = 2048
prompt              = no
default_md          = sha256
distinguished_name = dn
req_extensions      = req_ext
[dn]
C = IN
ST = Maharashtra
L = Mumbai
O = Example Org
CN = myapp.example.com
[req_ext]
subjectAltName = @alt_names
[alt_names]
DNS.1 = myapp.example.com
DNS.2 = www.myapp.example.com
```

Next, we then create the CSR with SANs:

```
openssl req -new -key server.key -out server.csr -config
csr.conf
```

Deploying Certificate Chains

Once the CA returns the certificate (like **server.crt**), we can try to receive one or more "intermediate" certificates. But to avoid browser or client warnings, we can always deploy the full chain.

Next, we then combine the server certificate and intermediate certificates into a single file:

```
cat server.crt intermediate.crt > fullchain.crt
```

Here, we place these files where the web or application server expects them. For example, in Nginx:

```
ssl_certificate /etc/ssl/certs/fullchain.crt;
ssl_certificate_key /etc/ssl/private/server.key;
```

And then, we reload or restart the service to apply the change.

Validating Hostname and Expiry

To check that the certificate matches the hostname and hasn't expired, we make use of:

```
openssl s_client -connect myapp.example.com:443 -servername
myapp.example.com
```

Here, we look for the "**Verify return code: 0 (ok)**" and check the CN and SAN fields match the hostname. Also, we look for the **notBefore** and **notAfter** dates to confirm the certificate is valid and not about to expire.

And, if we want a quick expiry check:

```
openssl x509 -in server.crt -noout -dates
```

We can also use browser developer tools or online checkers (like SSL Labs) to validate the chain and hostname.

Quick Smoke Test

Once deployed, we then hit the application from a client or browser. We should see the lock icon in the address bar, and clicking on it shows the certificate details. No errors, no warnings.

For CLI apps, if we get a successful output from **curl**, then it is a good sign:

```
curl -v https://myapp.example.com/
```

In its output, we then watch for "**SSL connection using**" and "**subject**" lines that confirm the new certificate is in use.

When we control the key, CSR, and full chain, we oversee trust, no last-minute surprises, no broken clients, and no late-night certificate fires. Each client-side check is the guarantee that the certificate works, protects, and verifies just as it should.

Opening Service Needs

Every port or protocol we leave open is a potential target. The most secure approach is to only allow the traffic the service needs, no more, no less. So, if we craft a targeted rule for each service, and checking that it's hit when needed, we can keep the system safe while letting business traffic flow. And, with zones (like in firewalld) or tables/chains (in nftables or iptables), we can be very specific about what is allowed, and from where.

Targeted Rules

We will let us consider that we are running a web service that only needs HTTP and HTTPS open to the public, and SSH only for the jump box at **192.168.10.10**.

Using firewalld zones

So here, we will first assign interfaces or sources to zones, and only open the ports required in each.

```
sudo firewall-cmd --zone=public --add-service=http --permanent
sudo firewall-cmd --zone=public --add-service=https --
permanent
```

Here, we will then allow SSH only from the jump box in the trusted zone:

```
sudo firewall-cmd --zone=trusted --add-source=192.168.10.10/32
--permanent
sudo firewall-cmd --zone=trusted --add-service=ssh --permanent
```

After this, we will then reload to apply:

```
sudo firewall-cmd --reload
```

Using nftables tables

Next, we then set up a filter table that only allows what's needed:

```
table inet filter {
  chain input {
    type filter hook input priority 0;
    iifname "eth0" tcp dport {80, 443} accept
    ip saddr 192.168.10.10 tcp dport 22 accept
    ct state established,related accept
    reject with icmpx type port-unreachable
  }
}
```

We then apply the ruleset with:

```
sudo nft -f /etc/nftables.conf
```

Verifying Counters

After adding the targeted rules, we can always check that the counters are increasing only for the traffic we want.

Like, for firewalld (nftables backend):

```
sudo nft list ruleset
```

here, we must watch the **`packets`** and **`bytes`** counts for each rule. And then we need to trigger a connection from the allowed client, and see the counters go up.

And, for iptables:

```
sudo iptables -L -n -v
```

We can spot which rule is being used by the bump in packet counts after each test.

Recording Endpoint Checks

We must note that we cannot just rely on counters. We must try to connect from allowed and denied sources.

So for this, we will test from allowed client:

```
ssh user@server   # From 192.168.10.10

curl -I http://server   # From any public client
```

In this, we should see the connection succeed. We must ensure to record these test results, both successes and failures, so we have solid evidence that the rules are as tight as promised.

Verifying Controls using Audit Trails

Someone on the team has finished a weekend patch cycle and updated the firewall and SSH configs. On Monday, the auditor will ask for proof of what was changed and when. The system logs have already been rotated, and there's no fancy monitoring tool in place. The team now needs a way to quickly show what changed, and that nothing else was touched and all sensitive configs stayed safe. We want simple habits and quick tools that work every time, even if nobody set up a central audit platform.

Creating Hashes

Whenever we adjust a sensitive file, maybe the firewall config, the sshd_config, or an AppArmor profile, we need to pause a moment to capture its state:

```
sha256sum /etc/ssh/sshd_config > sshd_config.sha256
```

Next time, we need to confirm that nothing has drifted:

```
sha256sum -c sshd_config.sha256
```

If the file is unchanged, we get a clean "OK." If not, we spot the drift instantly. Do this for every file we know matters: sudoers, AppArmor, SELinux, or any config we cannot risk losing track of.

Recording Sensitive Edits

Every time we finish a change, write a quick, timestamped note, nothing fancy. So here, we will drop it into a plain log or audit file, like **`/var/log/security-audit.log`**:

```
echo "$(date '+%Y-%m-%d %H:%M') Changed sshd_config: disabled
root login for all users" | sudo tee -a /var/log/security-
audit.log
```

If the edit is big or needs more context, drop in the diff right after:

```
diff -u /etc/ssh/sshd_config.bak.20240721 /etc/ssh/sshd_config
| tee -a /var/log/security-audit.log
```

Over time, this simple file becomes the story, a visible trail that proves exactly who changed what, when, and why.

Audit Notes for Security Operations

For audit, a simple plain Markdown file or even a text note, shared with the team or kept alongside the project, is often all we need. So here, for each action, we will just add a line like:

```
2024-07-21 13:42 Updated firewall to block unused ports,
checked with endpoint probes, saved hash.
```

If we are working on a repo, we will keep these notes in the docs. If not, just store them in a spot the team trusts.

Overall, we don't need a big monitoring stack; just a few daily habits keep every system both tight and observable.

Knowledge Exercise

1. Before changing **`/etc/ssh/sshd_config`**, what is the best first step to enable a safe rollback?

   A. Copy the file to a backup or commit to version control

   B. Restart sshd immediately

   C. Remove all comments from the file

2. We apply a new AppArmor profile for a custom app and users report denied access. What's the most direct way to spot the problem?

   A. Check audit logs for denied messages

   B. Restart the system

   C. Delete the profile

3. A teammate disables password authentication in **`sshd_config`**. What command helps us record the exact state for future verification?

   A. **`sha256sum /etc/ssh/sshd_config > sshd_config.sha256`**

   B. **`cat /etc/ssh/sshd_config`**

C. **`chmod 600 /etc/ssh/sshd_config`**

4. We are deploying a new web server certificate. Which OpenSSL command verifies the hostname and expiry from the client side?

   A. **`openssl s_client -connect mysite.com:443 -servername mysite.com`**

   B. **`openssl req -new -key server.key -out server.csr`**

   C. **`openssl genpkey -algorithm RSA -out server.key`**

5. We want to allow HTTP and HTTPS to everyone, but SSH only from the admin subnet, using firewalld zones. What command allows SSH from just **`192.168.10.0/24`**?

   A. **`firewall-cmd --zone=trusted --add-source=192.168.10.0/24 --permanent`**

   B. **`firewall-cmd --zone=public --add-service=ssh --permanent`**

   C. **`firewall-cmd --zone=public --remove-service=ssh --permanent`**

6. A user says they can't access a service after a firewall change. Which tool helps us check if the right rule is matched?

   A. **`sudo nft list ruleset`** or **`sudo iptables -L -n -v`**

   B. **`df -h`**

   C. **`chage -l user`**

7. We want to record every sensitive edit in a simple audit log. Which shell command appends a timestamped message to the audit file?

   A. **`echo "$(date '+%Y-%m-%d %H:%M') Changed sudoers for projectX" | sudo tee -a /var/log/security-audit.log`**

   B. **`history > /var/log/security-audit.log`**

   C. **`chmod 700 /var/log/security-audit.log`**

8. We just applied a strict SELinux policy and the app will not start. What is the best rollback move?

   A. Restore the previous policy or config from backup or git

   B. Reboot twice

   C. Run the app as root

9. When issuing a new certificate, which config field must match the service's hostname to avoid client errors?

A. Common Name (CN) and Subject Alternative Name (SAN)

B. Organization Name

C. State or Province

10. After updating firewall and SSH settings, how do we quickly prove nothing drifted without heavy tools?

A. Compare current hashes to saved ones and check the audit notes

B. Scan the system for open ports

C. Run **`ps aux`**

Note: In this chapter quiz, option A is the correct answer for every question.

CHAPTER 7: SHELL SCRIPTING AND TINY PYTHON UTILITIES

Every Linux system grows in its own way, with manual tweaks, quick config changes, and hotfixes layered on top of each other. Over time, these small differences pile up and make troubleshooting slow and risky. Whether we are maintaining a handful of servers or hundreds, it gets harder to answer simple questions like, "Are all hosts really set up the same way?" or "Did our config drift since the last patch?" This is where scripting steps in, not as a replacement for standard tools, but as the glue that keeps the environment predictable. With just a bit of Bash or Python, we can make quick fixes, enforce settings, and give the team the proof that every system is right, without the fear of breaking what already works.

This chapter focuses on writing small, safe scripts that do what we want, skip what's already right, and always leave a clear trail.

Writing Idempotent Bash Fixers

Let us assume, that we get a ticket about sudoers settings drifting across the servers. Some systems have passwordless sudo, some prompt for a password, and others are missing the right group entirely. Someone suggests "just run a script everywhere," but we know the risk: a naive script can break sudo access, lock out users, or keep flipping settings every run. What we need is a Bash fixer that only makes changes when needed, always shows what happened, and proves to the team (and yourself) that it's safe to run again and again.

Creating Idempotent Scripts

An idempotent script is one that checks the current state before it acts. If everything is already right, it quietly exits. If not, it fixes only what's broken. Following is an example for fixing a line in **/etc/sudoers** to require a password for the **admin** group, with proof:

```
#!/bin/bash
set -e
TARGET_LINE='%admin ALL=(ALL:ALL) ALL'
SUDOERS_FILE='/etc/sudoers'
if grep -Fxq "$TARGET_LINE" "$SUDOERS_FILE"; then
  echo "PASS: Sudoers already correct."
else
  echo "FIX: Sudoers not correct, applying fix."
  cp "$SUDOERS_FILE" "$SUDOERS_FILE.bak.$(date +%Y%m%d%H%M%S)"
  echo "$TARGET_LINE" >> "$SUDOERS_FILE"
fi
```

```
if grep -Fxq "$TARGET_LINE" "$SUDOERS_FILE"; then
  echo "PASS: Sudoers fixed."
else
  echo "FAIL: Could not fix sudoers."
  exit 1
fi
```

The script checks for the exact line. If it is already there, we get a "PASS" message. If not, it backs up the file, adds the line, and then asserts the result. Every run is safe, if the setting is already present, nothing changes.

Including Asserts

We then build the scripts so they always finish by checking if the fix really worked. Each key step emits either "PASS" or "FAIL," making the outcome obvious.

So next, we add the asserts to confirm settings. For example, after making a firewall change:

```
sudo ufw allow 80
if sudo ufw status | grep -q '80/tcp'; then
  echo "PASS: Port 80 allowed."
else
  echo "FAIL: Port 80 not allowed."
fi
```

These checks show exactly what was done (or skipped), so there's never a silent failure or a "did this even run?" mystery.

Next, we will run the fixer script with logging enabled, and save output to a proof file:

```
sudo ./fix-sudoers.sh | tee fixer-output.log
```

This creates an instant record for the own peace of mind, and for teammates or auditors who need to see the proof. The result is a team that trusts the scripts and a system state we can prove, not just hope for.

Creating One-Page Incident Summaries

Something unexpected goes wrong with the service and it affects production late in the evening.

The logs are massive, with thousands of lines per minute across a bunch of systems. The team needs answers to the following questions: what actually broke, how often, and which events matter most? We want to create a one-page incident summary quickly, without getting overwhelmed by raw log data or endless scrolling.

Extracting Events using 'grep' and 'awk'

At first, we start by pulling out just the log lines related to the incident. For example, say the service is called **myapp** and errors always contain the word "ERROR".

```
grep 'ERROR' /var/log/myapp.log > errors.log
```

Or, if we want a time window (let's say between 13:00 and 14:00):

```
awk '$0 ~ /2024-07-21 13:/' /var/log/myapp.log | grep 'ERROR'
> errors-13-14.log
```

We can also look for repeated failure messages, authentication problems, or timeouts, change the keyword as needed.

For example, to quickly see counts by error type:

```
awk -F':' '{print $4}' errors.log | sort | uniq -c | sort -nr
```

We then adjust the field based on the log's structure.

Grouping Events

Next, we then must group the extracted lines to show what caused the issue, and when spikes happened.

So, to group by cause (the actual error message):

```
awk -F'ERROR' '{print $2}' errors.log | sort | uniq -c | sort
-nr > error-summary.txt
```

This creates a count of each unique error. You'll instantly see which problems were most frequent.

To group by time:

If the logs start with timestamps like **2024-07-21 13:42:19**, grab the minute or hour:

```
awk '{print substr($1,1,13)}' errors.log | sort | uniq -c |
sort -nr > errors-by-minute.txt
```

This gives us the error count per minute or hour, helping us spot spikes or patterns.

Producing Machine-Readable Outputs

Now, we will create a one-page summary for people by combining top causes and timeline spikes. For a human summary, we can use simple headings and short tables:

```
Incident: Service Outage
Date: 2024-07-21
Time Range: 13:00 to 14:00
Top Error Types:
  120  Database connection timeout
   45  Authentication failed
   17  API rate limit exceeded
Error Spikes By Minute:
  38  2024-07-21 13:25
  29  2024-07-21 13:26
  22  2024-07-21 13:40
```

For machine-readable summaries, the output is as CSV:

```
awk -F'ERROR' '{print $1 "," $2}' errors.log > incident-summary.csv
```

This approach means we can walk into a war room or drop a summary into chat, and everyone instantly sees the who, what, and when, no raw log slogging needed. If someone asks for proof, we have both the filtered logs and the counts grouped by cause and time, ready to share or feed into an automation.

Parsing JSON using Micro Python Helper

Sometimes you're handed an API response, a log dump or a config file in JSON format. Maybe it's a Kubernetes status, a cloud billing report, or a monitoring webhook. It's got loads of fields, but we only need a few: a status, an ID, maybe a timestamp. Searching for text is a bit unreliable, and scrolling by hand is just a waste of time. What we need is a tiny Python helper that can filter for exactly what matters, spit out just the summary, and always exit cleanly, so this can plug into any larger script or pipeline.

Reading JSON and Filtering Keys

For this, we first start with a small, reusable Python script. Let's call it **json_filter.py**. The idea is to read JSON from a file or standard input, pull out only the keys we want, and print a clean summary.

Following is a sample script:

```
#!/usr/bin/env python3
import sys
import json
# List of keys to extract
KEYS = ["status", "id", "timestamp"]
try:
    data = json.load(sys.stdin)
    # If it's a list, work on each item; if not, just process the dict
    items = data if isinstance(data, list) else [data]
    for item in items:
        summary = {k: item.get(k) for k in KEYS if k in item}
        print(summary)
    sys.exit(0)
except Exception as e:
    print(f"FAIL: {e}", file=sys.stderr)
    sys.exit(1)
```

Using Helper Script

We can have a file called **api_response.json**:

```
[
  {"status": "ok", "id": "alpha", "timestamp": "2024-07-22T10:20:00Z", "detail": "Success"},
  {"status": "fail", "id": "beta", "timestamp": "2024-07-22T10:21:00Z", "detail": "Timeout"}
]
```

And, we can run the script like this:

```
cat api_response.json | ./json_filter.py
```

Following is the desired output:

```
{'status': 'ok', 'id': 'alpha', 'timestamp': '2024-07-22T10:20:00Z'}
{'status': 'fail', 'id': 'beta', 'timestamp': '2024-07-22T10:21:00Z'}
```

Emitting Compact Summaries

The script always tries to print only the keys we care about. If something is missing or goes wrong (bad JSON, missing fields), it prints a clear FAIL message and exits with a nonzero code. That way, if we plug this script into a larger pipeline, we can check **$?** to see if it ran cleanly.

We can expand the script to support key filtering from the command line, or output as CSV or JSON Lines for further processing.

Following is the example for a custom run:

```
cat api_response.json | ./json_filter.py > summary.log
if [ $? -eq 0 ]; then
  echo "PASS: JSON parsed cleanly."
else
  echo "FAIL: JSON parse failed."
fi
```

This pattern means we never need to grep raw JSON again. It will always give us a clear, minimal summary, easy for a person to read, and even easier to feed into the next script or audit process.

Packaging Reuse Scripts

Generally, there is a handy script needed to automate a server fix, parse some logs, or patch a config. But after some time, someone asked, "How do I run this?" or "What does this flag do?" Maybe they use the wrong arguments or miss the log file, and we spend time supporting the own code. To save everyone time and make scripts a team asset, we want each script to be self-explaining, easy to call with flags, and clear about success or failure. The goal here is to have a script that anyone can reuse, without a live demo or hand-holding.

Standardizing Flags and Return Values

For this, we will look at an example of Bash first. We will add support for **-h** or **--help**, and use **-o** for output files or **-v** for verbose logging.

```
#!/bin/bash
set -e
usage() {
  echo "Usage: $0 [-f input_file] [-o output_file] [-v] [-h]"
  echo ""
  echo "  -f    Input file to process"
  echo "  -o    Output file to write"
  echo "  -v    Enable verbose mode"
  echo "  -h    Show help and exit"
}
VERBOSE=0
INPUT=""
OUTPUT=""
while getopts ":f:o:vh" opt; do
  case ${opt} in
    f ) INPUT=$OPTARG ;;
    o ) OUTPUT=$OPTARG ;;
    v ) VERBOSE=1 ;;
    h ) usage; exit 0 ;;
    \?) usage; exit 1 ;;
  esac
done
if [ -z "$INPUT" ]; then
  echo "FAIL: No input file given."
  usage
  exit 2
```

```
fi
if [ $VERBOSE -eq 1 ]; then
  echo "Reading from $INPUT, writing to $OUTPUT"
fi
# Main logic goes here
if [ -n "$OUTPUT" ]; then
  echo "PASS: Processing complete." > "$OUTPUT"
else
  echo "PASS: Processing complete."
fi
exit 0
```

Adding Tiny Help Block

Next, we then put a help block near the top. Even if someone opens the script in a text editor, it should take just seconds to see how to use it. The Python also works the same way:

```
#!/usr/bin/env python3
import argparse
import sys
def main():
    parser = argparse.ArgumentParser(
        description="Parse a log file and summarize error 
counts."
    )
    parser.add_argument("-f", "--file", help="Input file", 
required=True)
    parser.add_argument("-o", "--output", help="Output file")
    parser.add_argument("-v", "--verbose", 
action="store_true")
    args = parser.parse_args()
    if args.verbose:
```

```
        print(f"Processing {args.file}")
    # Main logic here...
    if args.output:
        with open(args.output, 'w') as fout:
            fout.write("PASS: Done\n")
    else:
        print("PASS: Done")
    sys.exit(0)
if __name__ == "__main__":
    main()
```

Standardizing Logs and Return Codes

The scripts always log what happened and where. So when possible, we must print key results or errors to both the terminal and a log file, using timestamps. For example, we can use:

- **`exit 0`** for success (PASS)
- **`exit 1`** or another nonzero code for failure (FAIL)
- Consistent "PASS" or "FAIL" lines in logs, so other scripts or teammates can parse results easily

If something goes wrong, print the message and exit with the right code. For Bash:

```
if [ ! -f "$INPUT" ]; then
  echo "FAIL: Input file not found." >&2
  exit 1
fi
```

With these habits, standard flags, clear help, always logging outcomes, and adding usage examples, the scripts become reusable by anyone, even months later. The newer teammates get answers right from the script itself, and other scripts can call yours knowing exactly what to expect in return codes and output.

Knowledge Exercise

1. Which script design ensures repeated runs never break the system or repeat unnecessary

changes?

A. Idempotent scripts that check state before acting

B. Scripts with hard-coded values

C. Cron jobs that run every minute regardless of status

2. We want the Bash script to show clear results for each action. Which approach best supports this?

A. Use “PASS” or “FAIL” lines after every critical step

B. Suppress all output

C. Only print results to a file

3. When summarizing logs for an incident, what is the most efficient way to extract all error lines for a service called **dbsync**?

A. **grep 'ERROR' /var/log/dbsync.log**

B. **ls -l /var/log/**

C. **cp /var/log/dbsync.log**

4. Which tool or combination is best for grouping log events by time and cause in a one-page incident summary?

A. **awk** and **sort | uniq -c**

B. **cat** and **wc -l**

C. **chmod** and **find**

5. We are writing a Python script to process JSON data. How can we ensure only the required keys are included in the output?

A. Filter the keys in code and emit only needed fields

B. Print the full JSON regardless

C. Use **grep** on the raw file

6. After running the JSON micro-helper, we want to confirm it succeeded before using its output. Which practice works best?

A. Check the exit code and only proceed if it is zero

B. Rerun the script several times

C. Ignore errors and parse the output blindly

7. We want to standardize script usage for the team. What is the most user-friendly approach?

A. Add standard flags like **-h** for help and include usage examples

B. Only accept positional arguments with no help text

C. Require users to read the source code to understand flags

8. How do we make sure a Bash or Python script always logs outcomes in a way that can be parsed by people and machines?

A. Use consistent "PASS" or "FAIL" statements and standard log files

B. Print only to stdout with no structure

C. Only email the results to the script's author

9. Which of the following is a reliable way to allow teammates to reuse the script with minimum confusion?

A. Store usage examples at the bottom or in a README, with clear flag explanations

B. Leave all documentation out and answer questions case-by-case

C. Make the script interactive only

10. In a Bash fixer script, how can we back up a config before making changes for safe rollback?

A. Use **`cp file file.bak.$(date +%Y%m%d%H%M%S)`** before editing

B. Delete the file if not needed

C. Only rely on the undo command

Note: In this chapter quiz, option A is the correct answer for every question.

CHAPTER 8: ANSIBLE AND GIT FOR OPS

These days, operations teams are all about automation. Whether we're handling a few servers or a whole fleet in different clouds, no one wants to keep making manual fixes, risking typos, or guessing if a patch has actually made it everywhere. Ansible and Git are two of the best tools we've got. With Ansible, we can write simple, readable plays that enforce the exact state we want, every time. With Git, we've got a solid record of who changed what and when. When we put these tools together, infrastructure becomes something we can understand, with code that's tracked, tested and always ready to roll back if needed.

In this chapter, we'll take a look at recipes that make these tools second nature, from writing minimal Ansible plays to building real CI/CD pipelines for the operational tasks.

Installing, Templating and Restarting

A small web service needs to be set up on each host. The requirements are pretty straightforward: install the right package (like nginx or httpd), deploy a templated configuration file tailored for each environment, and restart the service if the config changes. I'm not a fan of manual installs, and one-off scripts can get messy fast. What we're after is an Ansible playbook that any team member can run, and one that always delivers the same outcome every time. We want it to be installed, configured and running with a proof trail in every step.

Delivering Three-Task Play

To begin with, we will first build the Ansible play step by step, keeping it clean and showing proof at every stage.

```
- name: Ensure nginx is installed
  ansible.builtin.package:
    name: nginx
    state: present
```

This task checks if nginx is already present. If it is, nothing changes; if not, Ansible installs it. We always know the result, and it's safe to run again and again.

Next, we then need to render the template. Suppose we have a config file like **`nginx.conf.j2`** (Jinja2 template) in the playbook's **`templates`** directory. This template can use variables (like environment names or custom ports).

```
- name: Deploy nginx configuration from template
  ansible.builtin.template:
    src: nginx.conf.j2
```

```
    dest: /etc/nginx/nginx.conf
    owner: root
    group: root
    mode: '0644'
  notify: Restart nginx
```

If Ansible finds that the rendered config is different from what's on disk, it replaces it. If not, nothing happens. The **notify** triggers a handler only if there's a real change.

Next, we then will be restartarting through the handler. A handler is just a special task that runs only when notified, here, only if the config file actually changed.

```
handlers:
  - name: Restart nginx
    ansible.builtin.service:
      name: nginx
      state: restarted
```

This way, nginx never restarts unless it needs to. Your playbook always leaves the system in the correct state, with the smallest possible impact.

Running Play

Finally, when we run the playbook, the Ansible reports every change, skipped step, and handler run right in the output. We can see exactly what was done, on every host.

```
ansible-playbook deploy_nginx.yml
```

The summary will tell us which tasks changed the system and which were already perfect. That's the proof, readable, repeatable, and safe to show anyone on the team.

In all, with just three tasks, we can have a successfully delivered installation, templating, and a clean restarts, all tracked and controlled by Ansible.

Rendering Safe Templates

Let us think that we're updating a config template for nginx, PostgreSQL, or a monitoring tool. It's not always necessary to change ports, hostnames or log settings, but it's best to stick with the company's safe defaults. Even worse, there are sensitive secrets (like database passwords or API keys) mixed in, and we want to make sure they never end up in version control or debug output.

So, we'll show exactly what's different and prove that the template passes a quick lint and test before we roll out any changes.

Adding Sensible Defaults

In the Ansible templates (Jinja2), we will first define safe, predictable defaults for every variable that could be unset. For example, in **nginx.conf.j2**:

```
server {
    listen {{ nginx_port | default(80) }};
    server_name {{ nginx_server_name | default('localhost')
}};
    access_log {{ nginx_access_log |
default('/var/log/nginx/access.log') }};
    # ...other settings...
}
```

This means that unless someone overrides **nginx_port**, **nginx_server_name**, or **nginx_access_log**, they'll always get values we trust. No "undefined variable" errors, and no surprises in the config.

Protecting Secrets

One thing you should always bear in mind is that you should never use secrets in templates. Instead, use Ansible Vault or external secret management, and always reference secrets with variables:

```
db_password={{ db_password }}
```

In the playbook, supply secrets using vault files, encrypted variables, or CI/CD pipeline injection:

```
vars_files:
  - vault.yml  # Encrypted file holding db_password
```

We can also add logic in the template to block the config from rendering if a secret is missing:

```
{% if db_password is not defined %}
  # ERROR: db_password not set!
{% else %}
```

```
  db_password={{ db_password }}
{% endif %}
```

Linting Templates

Before deploying a new template, we must always lint it for syntax errors:

```
ansible-playbook --syntax-check site.yml
```

Next, we then test the rendering of the template locally:

```
ansible localhost -m template -a "src=nginx.conf.j2
dest=/tmp/nginx.conf"
```

We can also use **ansible-lint** to catch common errors or security mistakes.

Attaching Clean Diff

Finally, every time we roll out a new config, we then attach a diff showing exactly what changed. The Ansible shows diffs by default when running with the **--diff** flag:

```
ansible-playbook site.yml --diff
```

Here, you can see a colorized output with only the lines that changed, making it easy for a reviewer (or future you) to spot real differences and audit quickly.

Rolling Back using Tags and Git

Now here, let us assume that we have deployed a fresh config or codebase to the servers from a Git repo, but something critical broke. And, maybe the new nginx config crashed the service, or a new handler in the Ansible playbook took down part of production. The team members are asking how fast we can get back to a stable, working state, and everyone wants to know that the fix really worked. This is where Git tags save the day, letting us pin, revert, and verify, so recovery is never guesswork.

Pinning Known-Good Tag

Before every big rollout, we then tag the repo at a "golden" state:

```
git tag prod-2024-07-22
git push --tags
```

This tag marks exactly what was working. If a change goes wrong later, we have a reference point to roll back to with zero guesswork.

Rolling Back

If the new config or playbook causes trouble, we then simply check out the last known-good tag:

```
git fetch --tags
git checkout prod-2024-07-22
```

After this, we can now have the files, configs, or playbooks set exactly as they were at that safe point. And then, we deploy them to the servers or rerun the automation as needed.

For example, with Ansible:

```
ansible-playbook site.yml
```

Or, if we are using a config managed by Git:

```
sudo cp nginx.conf /etc/nginx/nginx.conf
sudo systemctl restart nginx
```

Rerunning Verifier

Once we have rolled back, we must ensure that the things are fixed. For this, we will rerun whatever verification we have:

Such as, for a web service, we will do:

```
curl -I http://your-server
```

and look for **`HTTP/1.1 200 OK`**.

For Ansible, we will simply check the summary output for "ok" and "changed" lines.

For a service, we will use:

```
systemctl status nginx
```

Each of the test gives us real evidence the rollback succeeded.

As soon as the service is up and healthy again, let the team know, attach the output from the verifier, the Git tag used, and the time of rollback. Example message:

```
Rolled back to prod-2024-07-22, nginx restarted, curl check passed (HTTP 200). System healthy as of 11:48 AM.
```

This habit not only saves hours during incidents but builds trust, everyone knows there's a clear, safe way to undo risky changes, and that every recovery can be proven, not just hoped for.

Developing Configuration History

Intent-based Committs

Here, we start every commit with a clear intent. Instead of vague messages like "update config" or "fixes," we just write exactly what changed and why:

```
git add nginx.conf

git commit -m "Switch nginx access logs to JSON format for log aggregator compatibility"
```

This habit means that when you, a teammate, or an auditor look back, every change tells a clear story. If we update a handler, tweak a template, or fix a port, mention the reason. Over time, the history reads like a narrative, not a jumble.

Next, when automating with playbooks, we commit changes to both the templates and the Ansible roles in sync:

```
git add templates/nginx.conf.j2 roles/web/tasks/main.yml

git commit -m "Increase worker_connections in nginx and update Ansible handler to restart service"
```

By doing this, we are not just recording what we did, but why we did it and how different files or actions are related.

Tagging Stable States

Whenever we reach a point where the configuration or playbook is known to work, set a tag. We make use of descriptive names, and push tags so the whole team (and any automation) can use them as below:

```
git tag stable-2024-07-22

git push --tags
```

The tags are the bookmarks for quick rollbacks or audits. Anyone can fetch the repo and check out a stable state:

```
git fetch --tags
git checkout stable-2024-07-22
```

If the workflow uses continuous integration or deployments, we can use the tags to trigger releases and record exactly what was shipped.

Including Micro Check Scripts

For every significant change, we can attach a tiny check script, could be Bash, Python, or even a simple Markdown test plan. These scripts are emant to verify the intent of the commit, such as:

- If we changed a config, the script might curl the endpoint and check for an expected header or response.
- If we updated a firewall, the script might attempt a connection on the port to prove it's open or closed.
- If we altered an Ansible playbook, a test could run the playbook in **--check** mode and confirm idempotence.

So, for example, if we bump a version or change a template:

```
# check_nginx_json_logs.sh
curl -s http://localhost/nginx_status | grep
"log_format.*json"
```

When every commit is purposeful, every stable state is tagged, and every big change comes with a micro-check, the configuration repo turns into a living playbook. It's not just history, it's a reproducible manual for recovery, troubleshooting, and audits. Anyone on the team, even months later, can replay exactly what happened and verify that the system is working as promised.

Knowledge Exercise

1. Which Ansible module is best for ensuring a package is installed on a target system?
   A. **ansible.builtin.package**
   B. **ansible.builtin.copy**
   C. **ansible.builtin.command**
2. In an Ansible playbook, how do we ensure a service restarts only if its configuration file changes?

A. Use a handler triggered by the **`notify`** keyword in the template task

B. Add a **`restart`** command to every task

C. Call the service restart in a pre-task

3. Which template variable pattern in Jinja2 sets a default value if none is provided?

A. **`{{ variable | default('value') }}`**

B. **`{{ variable or 'value' }}`**

C. **`{{ 'value' if not variable }}`**

4. What is the safest way to store sensitive secrets, such as passwords, in an Ansible project?

A. Use Ansible Vault or encrypted variable files

B. Hardcode secrets directly in templates

C. Send secrets in plaintext emails

5. Which **`ansible-playbook`** flag provides a line-by-line diff of what changed during a run?

A. **`--diff`**

B. **`--check`**

C. **`--list-tasks`**

6. After a failed deployment, how can we quickly restore a known-good configuration with Git?

A. Check out the last stable tag and redeploy

B. Reinstall the operating system

C. Manually edit configuration files on each server

7. Why should every commit message in a configuration repository be written with clear intent?

A. To ensure history is easy to audit, replay, and understand

B. To reduce the number of lines in the repo

C. To make the repo look bigger for compliance

8. When managing Ansible and config files with Git, why is it important to tag stable states?

A. Tags allow fast rollbacks and mark tested releases

B. Tags delete old branches

C. Tags hide sensitive files

9. What's the main benefit of including a small test or check script in each major commit?

A. It lets anyone verify the change works as intended

B. It increases the file count

C. It makes the repo larger for compliance

10. How does running an Ansible playbook show proof that a system is in the desired state?

    A. The playbook output lists all changes, skipped steps, and handler runs for every host

    B. Ansible hides all output for security

    C. Playbooks never display changes

Note: In this chapter quiz, option A is the correct answer for every question.

Chapter 9: Troubleshooting and Observability

Things like stuttering production or a slow server can be a bit of a panic, but having a clear picture of what's going on is the best way to deal with it. These days, Linux systems run loads of services, deal with sudden surges in demand and are controlled by automation until something goes wrong and the phone rings. If we're dealing with a sudden outage, a slow database or a user saying "the site is down", we need to be able to troubleshoot fast and fix things quickly. This is the best way to save downtime and build trust.

This chapter looks at real-world habits for observability and diagnosis. We'll use the tools that come with every Linux distribution, work through narrowing down the root cause step by step, and build confidence by always repeating the measure after any fix.

Spotting CPU, Memory, I/O & Socket Pressure

So it's mid-morning and support has flagged a web app running slow. There's no error message, just spinning loaders. The monitoring page shows everything's fine, but I just have a feeling something's wrong. With so many moving parts, we need a way to figure out:

- Is this a CPU overload?
- Memory running low?
- Is Disk I/O stuck? Or
- maybe the open sockets are maxed out?

The faster we work out what the main problem is, the sooner our users get their speed back.

Scanning CPU and Memory using 'top'

So, to begin with, we first fire up the **top** for an instant, live view of what's happening:

```
top
```

In this, we will watch the CPU usage. If a process is running at or near 100%, we will see it right at the top. We will examine the load averages too. If the numbers much higher than the CPU core count mean the system is overwhelmed.

For memory, we will check the "%MEM" column and look at "free" and "available" in the summary. And, if swap is in heavy use, it means memory is likely the bottleneck.

'vmstat' for Pressure Trends

The **vmstat 1 5** provides a rolling summary every second for five seconds:

```
vmstat 1 5
```

In the output, we will look for:

- High numbers in the "r" column: lots of runnable processes (CPU waiting)
- "si" and "so" (swap in/out): non-zero means memory pressure
- "wa" (I/O wait): consistently high shows disk I/O is slowing down the system

'iostat' for Disk Bottlenecks

If we are about to suspect the disks, then we will run:

```
iostat -xz 1 5
```

This will give us the extended stats, in which it will show us which device is busy. And in it, we will focus upon **%util** (numbers above 80% are a red flag), and **await** (high values mean requests are waiting on slow disks).

'ss' for Socket Saturation

Sometimes, it's the network, not the hardware. So here, we will run:

```
ss -s
```

This will give us a summary of socket use, including how many are in use or stuck. For more details, we will run:

```
ss -t state established | wc -l
```

This will count the open TCP connections. If this number is near system or service limits, it means we have found the culprit.

Applying Light Mitigation

Now, once we spot the likely bottleneck, such as if a runaway process is eating CPU, we then throttle or restart it.

```
renice +10 <pid>
kill <pid>
```

And, if the memory is tight, we then restart a leaky service or clear caches.

```
sudo systemctl restart myservice
sync; echo 3 | sudo tee /proc/sys/vm/drop_caches
```

After the action, we again then run the same commands and compare. This "fix and remeasure" habit is the best friend for confident troubleshooting and lasting improvement.

Tracing Stuck Process

Let us assume that sometime our monitoring flags a service as "running" but users are still waiting, maybe the web page never loads or the scheduled job never finishes. The process is alive, using little CPU, but appears frozen. So, in such case, we want to figure out exactly where it's stuck, capture the problem, and fix it, all without killing the process or causing a bigger outage.

Attaching 'strace' Samples

At first, we want to peek at what the process is doing, but we don't want to overwhelm it or the system. The **strace** will let us attach to a live process and watch its system calls for a few seconds.

So here, we will first find the process ID (PID):

```
ps aux | grep myapp
```

Let us assume that the PID is 1572. We will attach it with:

```
sudo strace -p 1572 -tt -T -f -o /tmp/strace-1572.out
```

We will let it run for about 5–10 seconds, then detach with **Ctrl+C**. This short window avoids big logs and keeps the impact minimal.

Capturing Blocking Call

We now open the strace output:

```
less /tmp/strace-1572.out
```

Next, we then scroll to the last lines. Here, we will look for calls that repeat or seem slow, often **read()**, **write()**, **connect()**, **accept()**, or **futex()**. If we see a long pause on a specific system call, or the same call repeating, that's usually where the process is stuck.

A typical sign is as below:

```
1572  10:42:13.248892 futex(0x7f2fa9e470c8, FUTEX_WAIT, 2,
NULL
```

If the process forks or uses threads, the **-f** flag ensures we catch child calls as well.

Fixing Condition

Once we spot the sticking point, we will then act directly on the root cause:

- If it's blocked waiting on a file, check disk space or file locks.
- If it's waiting for a network call, verify connectivity or service status at the other end.
- If it's locked on a mutex (**`futex`**), see if another process is holding the lock or deadlocked.

We can free up disk space, restart a dependent service, or resolve the network issue, often the stuck process will resume on its own as soon as the block clears.

Proving Fixes with Synthetic Checks

Maybe it was a config change, a hotfix or clearing a stuck process. The support team is watching for "all clear", so we need more than a hunch that things are working. It's possible that users won't spot the issue until later, so we need solid proof that key actions, logins, queries and data flows are working as they should. The best way to do this is to run synthetic checks, which are small scripts that mimic the real work the service does and capture their results.

Scripting Heartbeats and Small Transactions

A heartbeat check is a simple test that touches the application or service, often just with a ping or health endpoint:

```
curl -f http://localhost/healthz && echo "PASS: heartbeat" ||
echo "FAIL: heartbeat"
```

For a database:

```
psql -c 'SELECT 1;' && echo "PASS: db query" || echo "FAIL: db
query"
```

A small transaction check goes further. For a web app, we might log in, fetch a page, or perform a read/write test:

```
curl -s -X POST -d 'username=test&password=test'
http://localhost/login | grep 'Welcome' && echo "PASS: login"
|| echo "FAIL: login"
```

Or, for an API:

```
curl -s -H "Authorization: Bearer $TOKEN"
http://localhost/api/resource | jq .status | grep ok && echo
"PASS: api" || echo "FAIL: api"
```

We write these scripts so they return a "PASS" or "FAIL" string, and a nonzero exit code on failure. This makes them easy to call from cron, a CI job, or the own bash shell.

Running Checks

After we apply a fix, we then run the heartbeat and transaction scripts right away:

```
./heartbeat.sh | tee -a fix-check.log
./transaction_check.sh | tee -a fix-check.log
```

If we are rolling out a bigger change, keep running these scripts on a schedule (every minute or five) for the next 30–60 minutes. This helps catch any regressions or intermittent failures during the cooldown period.

For scheduled checks, we will run:

```
watch -n 60 './heartbeat.sh | tee -a fix-check.log'
```

Storing Outputs

Now, every time we run a synthetic check, save the output, timestamped, with all PASS/FAIL lines, so there's a record. This could be as simple as:

```
./heartbeat.sh >> /var/log/synthetic-checks.log
date >> /var/log/synthetic-checks.log
```

Or, for a group of checks, write results to a dedicated folder:

```
/checks/fix-2024-07-22/
    heartbeat.log
    api-check.log
    db-check.log
```

So, when someone asks, "Did it really work?" or "What was the state after that hotfix?" we can show the exact outputs, not just "it seemed fine at the time."

The synthetic checks give us active, repeatable proof that a service is healthy, not just after a fix, but whenever we need confidence. The combination of heartbeat and small transaction scripts means both the surface (is it up?) and the core (does it work?) are always covered.

Building Evidence Pack for Hand-Off

So, we have either finished a major troubleshooting sprint or we have gone for a risky config change. It worked, but now it's time to go off shift, hand things over to a teammate, or submit the fixes for review. The person who's done the job, the person who's in charge, or the next engineer needs more than just to hear that the job's finished. They want to see the trail: what was broken, what we did, and proof that the system is healthy now. The fastest way to do this is to gather everything into a small, self-contained evidence pack.

So here, we start by making a dedicated directory for the hand-off:

```
mkdir -p /tmp/evidence-pack-2024-07-22
```

Collect Key Logs

We copy over logs that show the incident and the recovery:

```
cp /var/log/syslog /tmp/evidence-pack-2024-07-22/
cp /var/log/myapp.log /tmp/evidence-pack-2024-07-22/
```

If we have got filtered or highlighted log snippets (like just the error window), include those too:

```
cp errors-incident.log /tmp/evidence-pack-2024-07-22/
```

Add Diffs and Change Proof

Next, we then include any config diffs that show exactly what changed:

```
diff -u config.old config.new > /tmp/evidence-pack-2024-07-22/config-change.diff
```

If we rolled back or redeployed with Git, add the **`git diff`** or the tag info:

```
git diff stable-2024-07-21..HEAD > /tmp/evidence-pack-2024-07-22/git-diff.txt
echo "Rolled back to tag: stable-2024-07-21" > /tmp/evidence-pack-2024-07-22/rollback-info.txt
```

Store Verification Results

After this, we then add output from every synthetic check, heartbeat, or test script we ran to prove the fix:

```
cp /checks/fix-2024-07-22/heartbeat.log /tmp/evidence-pack-2024-07-22/

cp /checks/fix-2024-07-22/api-check.log /tmp/evidence-pack-2024-07-22/
```

If we used **`curl`**, **`systemctl status`**, or any health endpoint, redirect the output:

```
curl -I http://localhost > /tmp/evidence-pack-2024-07-22/endpoint-status.txt

systemctl status myapp > /tmp/evidence-pack-2024-07-22/app-status.txt
```

Include README

And finally, we add a simple text file summarizing the incident, what was done, and what's in the pack:

```
Incident: Outage on 2024-07-22 at 14:17

Root cause: Exhausted memory, fixed by restarting service and clearing cache

Actions taken: See config-change.diff and git-diff.txt

Verification: All synthetic checks passed, logs and outputs included
```

And, we save this as **`/tmp/evidence-pack-2024-07-22/README.txt`**.

With everything bundled, logs, diffs, test results, and a quick summary, anyone picking up the hand-off knows exactly what happened and how we proved it's fixed. No need to hunt for emails, scroll through chat history, or guess what was done. If the same problem crops up again, this pack gives a shortcut straight to the solution.

Knowledge Exercise

1. A user reports a web app is slow. Which command helps us immediately identify high CPU or memory usage on the server?

A. **top**

B. **grep**

C. **date**

2. We want to spot disk I/O bottlenecks and see if the disks are saturated. Which tool do we run?

   A. **iostat -xz 1 5**

   B. **lsblk**

   C. **tar**

3. Which column in the **vmstat** output would we watch for high values if we suspect memory pressure?

   A. **si** and **so** (swap in and swap out)

   B. **bi** and **bo** (block in and out)

   C. **id** (CPU idle)

4. After fixing a suspected bottleneck, what should we do to prove the system is actually healthier?

   A. Rerun the same checks and compare results

   B. Log out and assume all is well

   C. Only ask users if it feels faster

5. Your service is running but appears frozen. What tool lets us safely see what system call it's stuck on?

   A. **strace -p <pid>**

   B. **kill -9 <pid>**

   C. **rsync**

6. We find a process stuck waiting on a file descriptor in strace output. What is a likely next troubleshooting step?

   A. Check the target of the file descriptor with **ls -l /proc/<pid>/fd/<fd>**

   B. Immediately reboot the server

   C. Ignore it and wait longer

7. After applying a fix, which method best proves that key actions work, not just that services are "up"?

   A. Run synthetic heartbeat and transaction scripts that test real workflows

B. Only check system uptime

C. View server temperature

8. What is the advantage of storing the output of the synthetic checks after a change or fix?

   A. Provides traceable proof of system health and successful remediation

   B. Takes up disk space with no benefit

   C. Slows down troubleshooting

9. We need to hand off a fixed incident to the next shift. What should we bundle into the minimal evidence pack?

   A. Key logs, diffs or change proof, verification outputs, and a summary README

   B. Only the personal notes

   C. A link to the documentation

10. Why is it valuable to include a short README in the evidence pack?

    A. It gives clear context on what happened, actions taken, and where to look for proof

    B. It is required for compliance even if empty

    C. It hides the details from the next person

Note: In this chapter quiz, option A is the correct answer for every question.

Chapter 10: Containers, Virtual Machines and Cloud-Init

These days, Linux operations don't have to be limited to physical servers or basic virtual machines. The latest teams are all about containers, orchestrating pods, spinning up virtual machines on demand, and using cloud-init to bring environments to life at boot. Although these technologies offer portability and speed, they also mean we have got more layers of troubleshooting to deal with. A container might disappear in seconds, a VM can misbehave after an image update, and a cloud-init script might silently skip key steps. In this chapter, we're going to look at the practical habits and quick checks that help us take control, no matter how much work there is.

Reviving Container

It's Monday morning and the development team has just delivered a new feature-packed Docker container. We pull the image, check the Compose file, and start it up expecting to see a web dashboard or API ready for testing. Instead, the container starts, flashes "Exited (1)" in the output, and vanishes in less than a second. The web page won't load and the container list in Docker only shows it with a short lifespan, no persistent process, no log output in the console, and no service listening on the expected port. At first, it's tempting to blame a bad image or network settings. But we remember this isn't the first time. Sometimes containers just disappear straight away because of a missing configuration, a required file that isn't mapped in, or an environment variable that hasn't been set. At other times, the entrypoint command fails, leaving only a cryptic message in the logs. It's all down to us now, so we need to get it up and running so we can start testing.

The only way forward is to see exactly what the container was trying to do, recreate the failure in a controlled way, and piece together what it needs to stay running. If the logs aren't clear or there's no interactive shell, we'll have to combine a few debugging habits, check the logs, look at the entry point and get a shell inside to find the fix and keep things moving.

Inspecting Logs and Entrypoint

We will start checking the container logs and pull the container ID:

```
docker ps -a
```

Then we will pull the logs:

```
docker logs <container-id-or-name>
```

In it, we will look for error messages, failed commands, or misconfigured environment variables. Often, the last line will hint at what crashed, maybe a missing file, a permission issue, or a failed startup command.

So next is, we will check what command the container is trying to run. For this, we will inspect the entrypoint and command:

```
docker inspect <container-id-or-name> | grep -i entrypoint
docker inspect <container-id-or-name> | grep -i cmd
```

This tells us exactly what the container is trying to execute when it starts.

Reproducing Interactively

Next, we will try to start the container in interactive mode with a shell so we can poke around:

```
docker run --rm -it <image-name> /bin/bash
```

or, if it's a minimal image:

```
docker run --rm -it <image-name> /bin/sh
```

If the shell launches, then we can say that we are inside the container and can look for missing files, and test environment variables. We can also manually run the startup command from the Dockerfile to see what fails:

```
cat /etc/os-release
ls /
env
./entrypoint.sh  # Or whatever the ENTRYPOINT or CMD is
```

If the shell exits immediately, the image may not have a shell installed or the ENTRYPOINT is overriding the command. For this, we will double-check the Dockerfile and try again.

Correcting Environment and Mapping Volumes

Very often, the containers exit because they're missing required environment variables or cannot find files they expect in a mounted volume. So for this, we will check the Dockerfile for **ENV** lines and required variables. And then, we will start the container with the correct variables:

```
docker run -e VAR1=value1 -e VAR2=value2 <image-name>
```

If files or folders are missing, we will map them in as volumes:

```
docker run -v /host/path:/container/path <image-name>
```

While we do this, we must be sure that the file paths and permissions match what the container expects. If an application needs a writable folder, set permissions on the host before running.

Remeasuring

After making corrections, we then start the container again normally:

```
docker run <image-name>
```

Most of the time, the containers that exit immediately just have a few small issues with their configuration, entry point or volume. If we inspect logs, attach interactively, and supply the right variables and mounts, we can debug unfamiliar images, bring up the workload, and document what fixed it for the next time.

Fixing Volume Permission Clashes

It's a container that mounts a directory from the host for persistent storage. At first, everything seems fine, but as soon as the application tries to write to that folder, we see errors like "Permission denied" in the logs. Maybe the web app can't create its log file, or the database container can't write to its data directory. The directory on the host has the right permissions for the regular user, but the container's process runs as a different UID. We can fix the permissions once, but the problem keeps coming back after every rebuild or restart. The only way to move forward is to match the UIDs between the host and the container, check from inside the container, and make sure the fix survives restarts.

Aligning UIDs

The core of this problem is that the files and directories on the host belong to one UID (for example, the user's UID is 1000), but the process inside the container might run as UID 999, 101, or something else. Docker (and Podman) do not remap permissions automatically.

So, to fix this:

Check UID of Host Directory

On the host, run:

```
ls -ln /path/to/volume
```

Here, we have to look at the UID (the number in the third column). Suppose it's **`1000`**.

Check UID inside Container

We then start the container with an interactive shell and the volume mounted:

```
docker run --rm -it -v /path/to/volume:/data <image-name>
/bin/bash
```

Once inside, we then check the UID the app uses:

```
id
ls -ln /data
```

If the UID inside the container does not match the host UID, that's the source of the clash.

Align UIDs

After this, on the host, we can chown the folder to match the container's expected UID. For example, if the container runs as UID 101:

```
sudo chown -R 101:101 /path/to/volume
```

Alternatively, we can run the container so the process inside uses the host UID:

```
docker run --rm -it -u $(id -u):$(id -g) -v
/path/to/volume:/data <image-name> /bin/bash
```

This confirms to us that all files created are matching the user's ownership.

Retesting from Container Within

After aligning UIDs, we then test the write access from inside the container:

```
echo "test" > /data/write-test.txt
cat /data/write-test.txt
```

If the file is created and readable, we can say to ourselves that we have fixed the clash.

If we ever rebuild the image or change the user the app runs as, we just need to remember to align the UID again. For team environments, we can document the required UID/GID in the README or the Docker Compose file.

Building, Tagging and Pushing Clean Image

We need someone to prepare a container image for a new internal tool. The code runs well on the machine, but now it's time to make the Dockerfile robust, build and tag the image with a clear version, push it to the team's local registry, and show another team member how to pull and use it on their own server. If we miss a detail, we risk shipping an image that's brittle, hard to track, or full of "works on my machine" issues.

Correcting Dockerfile

So, for this, we first start with the Dockerfile itself in which we will aim on clarity, repeatability, and minimal layers.

```
FROM python:3.11-slim
WORKDIR /app
COPY requirements.txt .
RUN pip install --no-cache-dir -r requirements.txt
COPY . .
CMD ["python", "main.py"]
```

If needed, we can lint the Dockerfile with **hadolint**, or at least we can run a review for accidental mistakes.

Tagging Consistently

A good tag tells us the version or intent, avoid "latest" unless we are actively developing. So for this, we will tag it correctly:

```
docker build -t mytool:1.0.0
```

We can tag for the registry directly:

```
docker tag mytool:1.0.0 localhost:5000/mytool:1.0.0
```

If the local registry runs at **localhost:5000**, make sure we always tag with the registry address so the next step works seamlessly.

Pushing to Local Registry

Next, we then start the local registry:

```
docker run -d -p 5000:5000 --name registry registry:2
```

After this, we then push the image:

```
docker push localhost:5000/mytool:1.0.0
```

In it, we will check the pushed image in the registry by listing the images.

Pulling Host

On another host, we will confirm if the Docker can reach the registry. Here, we will add the local registry address to the Docker daemon config for internal testing.

Then pull:

```
docker pull <your-registry-host>:5000/mytool:1.0.0
```

We then run the image to confirm it works:

```
docker run --rm -it <your-registry-host>:5000/mytool:1.0.0
```

If we get authentication or connection errors, we can at any given time can check the network or the firewall rules and the registry's settings.

With all this simple and easy steps, we are able to guarantee that the images are traceable and reproducible.

Unblocking Cloud-Init

We have just started up five new cloud VMs using our preferred platform, which may be OpenStack, AWS, Proxmox or KVM with a cloud-init ISO. As expected, one VM starts up and lets us log in. The others either refuse to accept the SSH key, skip the creation of the admin user or fail to install key packages. Rather than displaying any error messages, cloud-init simply skips a step and leaves us with an incomplete machine. Ideally, we would have a quick, repeatable checklist to identify where cloud-init failed, fix the problem and ensure the VMs are configured as intended.

Reading Cloud-Init Logs

If the SSH isn't working, we will try the cloud provider's web console, or attach to the VM on the host:

```
virsh console <vmname>
# or use AWS/Proxmox/VMware built-in console
```

After this, we then start with:

```
sudo tail -n 40 /var/log/cloud-init-output.log
```

```
sudo less /var/log/cloud-init.log
```

In it, we then look for lines like:

```
[ERROR] config-users-and-groups: Invalid YAML...
[WARNING] Failed to execute script...
```

Now here, we might spot YAML errors, failed **runcmd** scripts, or skipped modules.

Fixing Userdata

Next, we then download the userdata file, such as:

```
#cloud-config
users:
  - name: admin
    sudo: ALL=(ALL) NOPASSWD:ALL
    ssh_authorized_keys
      - ssh-rsa AAAAB3...
```

Now here, we will see that, it is missing a colon on **ssh_authorized_keys**, so cloud-init ignores the keys and sudo line!

For this, we will then validate the YAML, for which, we will run locally:

```
yamllint userdata.yaml
```

And then, we will correct the file. Following is a proper cloud-init snippet:

```
#cloud-config
users:
  - name: admin
    sudo: ['ALL=(ALL) NOPASSWD:ALL']
    ssh-authorized-keys:
      - ssh-rsa AAAAB3...
    shell: /bin/bash
runcmd:
```

```
  - echo "CLOUD INIT OK" > /tmp/cloud-ok.txt
```

Reapplying and Restarting

Finally, we will recreate the VM, or we will re-attach the fixed ISO/userdata.

```
openstack server create --user-data userdata.yaml ...
```

If the platform supports re-running cloud-init, we can also:

```
sudo cloud-init clean
sudo cloud-init init
sudo cloud-init modules --mode=config
sudo cloud-init modules --mode=final
```

This forces cloud-init to reprocess the fixed config.

Verifying Multi-Container Reachability

Now, our team has made good progress by deploying a multi-container stack, which may include a web front end, an API service and a database. All of these are defined in Compose or a Kubernetes YAML. Although everything appears to be functioning correctly, users may report issues such as the web app being unable to load data or the API failing to connect to the database. Furthermore, although health checks are green, traffic between containers may be blocked or volumes may not be mounted.

Overall, we need a fast and reliable way to confirm the port of every container, the internal network links and the storage. We also need to be able to identify and fix the first thing that fails and provide proof that everything is working properly.

Confirming Service Ports

So here, we will start with the basics. Like, we will check, if every container's main service listens on its expected port?

```
docker compose ps
```

Next, we then check that the **PORTS** column is as expected.

```
docker exec <container> ss -ltnp
```

This shows which ports are open and which processes own them.

Checking Container Links

From the "client" container, we then test if it can reach the "server" container on the expected port.

```
docker exec <web-container> curl -s http://api:8080/healthz
docker exec <api-container> curl -s http://db:5432/
```

If DNS or service names are used, then we confirm resolution:

```
docker exec <web-container> getent hosts api
```

If a connection fails, make a note of the error. If you see 'Connection refused', it means that the service is not listening. If you see 'Timeout', it means that there are network or DNS issues. If you see a 5xx error from an HTTP server, it means that the service is running, but not healthy.

Confirming Storage Claims

After this, we then check from inside any container that needs persistent storage:

```
docker exec <db-container> touch
/var/lib/postgresql/data/testfile && echo "PASS: storage
write"
docker exec <api-container> ls /mnt/data
```

If the writes fail, we then must check the volume mount in the Compose or pod YAML, and the permissions of the host path or PVC.

Capturing End-to-End Proof

After the fix, we then must repeat the curl or touch test. So, when it works, we then chain a single request from frontend to backend to database:

```
docker exec <web-container> curl -s http://api:8080/query?test
```

If the request travels all the way, web to API to DB, and gives the expected response, we then save that output as the "all-green" proof.

Knowledge Exercise

1. After running **`docker run <image>`**, the container exits immediately. What is the best first step?

A. Check the container logs and inspect the entrypoint
B. Delete the image and try again
C. Increase CPU limits

2. We mount a host directory into a container, but the application reports "Permission denied" on write. What is a likely fix?

   A. Align the host directory's UID/GID with the container's process user
   B. Make the directory world-writable without checking user IDs
   C. Remove the volume mount

3. Which **docker run** flag lets us start a container interactively for debugging file paths, permissions, or entrypoints?

   A. **-it**
   B. **-d**
   C. **--rm**

4. What is a recommended habit when tagging and pushing a new image to a local Docker registry?

   A. Tag with a clear version (not just **latest**) and include the registry address
   B. Only use **latest** and never specify the registry
   C. Push directly without checking the Dockerfile

5. After building and pushing an image to the local registry, how does a teammate pull and run it on their own machine?

   A. **docker pull <registry-host>:5000/<image>:<tag>** then **docker run <registry-host>:5000/<image>:<tag>**
   B. Email the image file to them
   C. Build the image from scratch on their own machine

6. We launch a VM with a cloud-init config, but can't SSH in and find the user missing. Which log file on the VM gives the clearest clue?

   A. **/var/log/cloud-init-output.log**
   B. **/etc/passwd**
   C. **/var/log/dmesg**

7. After correcting a cloud-init user-data YAML file, what step is necessary before we see the fix on a new VM?

   A. Re-create the VM with the fixed user-data file
   B. Only restart the SSH service
   C. Edit **/etc/shadow** manually

8. We want to confirm all containers in a multi-service stack can reach each other and use their storage. What combination of commands helps us check both networking and storage from

inside containers?

A. **`curl`** (or netcat) to service ports, and **`touch`** or **`ls`** in mounted volumes
B. Only run **`docker ps`**
C. Only restart all services

9. During multi-container troubleshooting, we find an API container cannot connect to the database, but both are "up." What is the first action?

A. Test network reachability and check connection details from inside the API container
B. Delete both containers and hope for success
C. Only check the host's firewall

10. After confirming reachability and fixing the smallest failing link in a multi-container app, what should we capture as proof of full-stack health?

A. A single end-to-end test result or log showing data flows through all services
B. A screenshot of the Docker Compose YAML
C. A backup of the host

Note: In this chapter quiz, option A is the correct answer for every question.

MOCK EXAM

SET 'A'

DOMAIN 1: System Architecture & Installation

1. Which command displays the system's boot messages on most modern distributions?

A. `dmesg`

B. `who`

C. `env`

D. `lastlog`

2. What does the runlevel 5 traditionally signify on a Red Hat-based system?

A. Multi-user without network

B. Single user

C. Halt

D. Multi-user with GUI

3. When we need to install a package and all its dependencies, which command should we use?

A. `rpm -ivh <package>.rpm`

B. `yum groupinstall <package>`

C. `apt install <package>`

D. `zypper addrepo <repo>`

4. To view all PCI devices in a system, which utility is best?

A. `lsof`

B. `lsblk`

C. `lspci`

D. `lsusb`

5. Which kernel boot parameter can be used to force a single-user mode on most distributions?

A. `safeboot`

B. `init=3`

C. `single`

D. `recovery`

6. Which file determines the default runlevel when using System V init?

A. `/etc/fstab`

B. `/boot/grub/grub.cfg`

C. `/etc/inittab`

D. `/etc/init.d/rc.local`

7. After running `lsmod`, we see a module is loaded but want to remove it. Which command is correct?

A. `depmod -a`

B. `rmmod <module>`

C. `insmod <module>`

D. `modprobe <module>`

8. Which action will NOT trigger an update to the kernel image?

A. Installing a new text editor

B. Running `apt full-upgrade` with new kernel available

C. Using `yum update` on kernel package

D. Compiling a new kernel

9. To change the default boot entry in GRUB2, which file should we edit?

A. `/etc/sysctl.conf`

B. `/etc/default/grub`

C. `/etc/initramfs-tools/modules`

D. `/etc/resolv.conf`

10. Which command lists all loaded kernel modules with their size and usage count?

A. `ls -l /lib/modules`

B. `lsmod`

C. `uname -r`

D. `modinfo`

11. Which environment variable determines the directory search order for executables?

A. `HOME`

B. `PATH`

C. `LANG`

D. SHELL

12. A user needs to see their shell's environment variables. Which command should they use?

A. df

B. export -p

C. env

D. hostname

13. You're building a kernel module from source. Which tool compiles it for the running kernel?

A. gcc

B. g++

C. cmake

D. make

DOMAIN 2: System Configuration & Management

14. Which command displays the scheduled jobs for the current user?

A. at -l

B. crontab -l

C. jobs

D. ls /etc/cron.*

15. To stop and prevent a systemd service from starting at boot, what two commands are required?

A. systemctl stop <service> and systemctl disable <service>

B. service <service> stop and chkconfig <service> off

C. systemctl reload <service> and systemctl enable <service>

D. initctl stop <service> and initctl disable <service>

16. Which log file contains authentication success and failure?

A. /var/log/secure

B. /var/log/messages

C. /var/log/syslog

D. `/var/log/auth.log`

17. We want to change the system time zone. What's the best approach on most distributions?

A. Edit `/etc/time.conf`

B. Use `timedatectl set-timezone <zone>`

C. Change `/etc/locale.conf`

D. Use `hwclock --set`

18. Which configuration file sets system-wide locale settings?

A. `/etc/localtime`

B. `/etc/locale.conf`

C. `/etc/issue`

D. `/etc/hosts`

19. What does the `hostnamectl` command NOT allow us to change?

A. Pretty hostname

B. Transient hostname

C. Static hostname

D. Network interface MAC address

20. Which tool displays hardware info, including CPU, memory, and BIOS, in a structured report?

A. `lsattr`

B. `lsmod`

C. `lshw`

D. `lsb_release`

21. Which field in `/etc/passwd` determines the user's login shell?

A. The fourth field

B. The last field

C. The second field

D. The third field

22. A user cannot log in because their shell is set to `/usr/sbin/nologin`. What command can we use to fix this?

A. usermod -s /bin/bash <user>

B. passwd <user>

C. groupmod <user>

D. chsh -l <user>

23. How do we test a new `/etc/sudoers` entry for syntax errors before applying it?

A. sudoers -t

B. sudo test

C. visudo -c

D. sudo --validate

24. What is the default location for user cron jobs?

A. /var/run/cron

B. /etc/crontab

C. /var/spool/cron/crontabs

D. /usr/local/cron

25. If a user's home directory is filling up, what command can summarize file and directory sizes in human-readable format?

A. du -h

B. ls -lah

C. stat -f

D. find . -ls

26. What utility would we use to find a package that provides a missing command?

A. whoami

B. apt-file search <command>

C. uname -a

D. modprobe -l

27. We want to see all systemd services that failed to start. Which command will show this?

A. systemctl list-units --type=socket

B. systemctl --failed

C. `journalctl -xe`

D. `service --status-all`

28. If we want to immediately apply changes to `/etc/sysctl.conf` without rebooting, which command should we run?

A. `sysctl -p`

B. `systemctl reload sysctl`

C. `reboot`

D. `sysctl -edit`

DOMAIN 3: Storage & Filesystems

29. Which command displays all block devices and their mount points?

A. `lsblk`

B. `lsmod`

C. `lsusb`

D. `blkid`

30. What utility initializes a physical disk for use with LVM?

A. `partprobe`

B. `pvcreate`

C. `mkfs`

D. `fdisk -l`

31. We want to see filesystem usage in a human-readable format. Which command should we use?

A. `ls -h`

B. `du --max-depth=1`

C. `df -h`

D. `mount -l`

32. How do we find the UUIDs for all mounted filesystems?

A. `mount`

B. `findmnt`

C. `blkid`

D. `cat /etc/mtab`

33. A user needs a temporary 512MB filesystem for build artifacts. Which one-liner achieves this?

A. `mkfs.ext4 /mnt/tmp`

B. `mount /mnt/tmp`

C. `dd if=/dev/zero of=/mnt/tmp bs=512M count=1`

D. `mount -t tmpfs -o size=512M tmpfs /mnt/tmp`

34. What option in `/etc/fstab` ensures a filesystem is not automatically mounted at boot?

A. `noauto`

B. `nofail`

C. `defaults`

D. `ro`

35. Which command sequence adds a new disk `/dev/sdd` to volume group `vgdata`?

A. `vgcreate vgdata /dev/sdd` and `lvcreate /dev/sdd`

B. `pvcreate /dev/sdd` and `vgextend vgdata /dev/sdd`

C. `fdisk /dev/sdd` and `partprobe`

D. `mkfs.ext4 /dev/sdd` and `mount /dev/sdd /data`

36. If we see "Input/output error" on a mounted filesystem, what is a likely immediate next step?

A. `chmod 777 /mnt`

B. `uptime`

C. `dmesg | tail`

D. `lsmod`

37. Which `mount` option makes `/tmp` world-writable but not executable?

A. `defaults,exec`

B. `noauto`

C. `ro`

D. `defaults,nosuid,noexec`

38. After creating a logical volume, which command grows an XFS filesystem to use all available space?

A. `resize2fs <mountpoint>`

B. `mkfs.xfs <device>`

C. `lvcreate -L`

D. `xfs_growfs <mountpoint>`

39. To migrate an existing ext4 filesystem to XFS, which is a correct procedure?

A. Use `tune2fs` to convert

B. Run `xfs_repair`

C. Backup, format with XFS, and restore

D. Run `xfs_admin`

40. What command lists NFS mounts currently in use?

A. `ls -nfs`

B. `mount -t nfs`

C. `df -h | grep nfs`

D. `lsnfs`

41. To reduce the size of a logical volume without data loss, what is the correct order?

A. Unmount, reduce LV, shrink FS

B. Grow LV, then shrink filesystem

C. Shrink filesystem, then reduce LV

D. Reduce LV, then shrink filesystem

DOMAIN 4: Security

42. What command locks a user account, disabling logins?

A. `passwd -l <user>`

B. `chsh <user>`

C. `usermod -d <user>`

D. `sudo -l <user>`

43. Which tool manages SELinux policy modules?

A. `chcon`

B. `semanage`

C. `getsebool`

D. `setsebool`

44. In `/etc/shadow`, what does an exclamation mark (!) at the start of a password field mean?

A. Account is locked

B. Password is empty

C. Account is root

D. Password never expires

45. Which command shows current sudo privileges for the current user?

A. `sudoedit`

B. `sudo -u`

C. `visudo`

D. `sudo -l`

46. We want to check the validity of the root user's authorized SSH keys. Which file do we inspect?

A. `/etc/ssh/ssh_config`

B. `/root/.ssh/authorized_keys`

C. `/etc/ssh/sshd_config`

D. `/home/root/ssh/authorized_keys`

47. What command adds an iptables rule to drop all incoming ICMP echo requests?

A. `iptables -A OUTPUT -p icmp --icmp-type echo-request -j DROP`

B. `iptables -A INPUT -p icmp --icmp-type echo-request -j DROP`

C. `iptables -A FORWARD -p icmp --icmp-type echo-request -j DROP`

D. `iptables -D INPUT -p icmp --icmp-type echo-request -j DROP`

48. Which method will quickly expire a user's password and force a change at next login?

A. `usermod -l 0 <user>`

B. `chage -d 0 <user>`

C. passwd -u <user>

D. passwd -l <user>

49. If SELinux is preventing web scripts from writing files, which context is usually needed?

A. user_home_t

B. var_log_t

C. tmp_t

D. httpd_sys_rw_content_t

50. Which command shows all firewall rules in the "public" zone using firewalld?

A. iptables -L

B. nft list ruleset

C. firewall-cmd --zone=public --list-all

D. ss -tlnp

51. What command displays recent failed login attempts on a system using journalctl?

A. journalctl _SYSTEMD_UNIT=sshd.service | grep "Failed password"

B. who -u

C. cat /var/log/auth.log

D. lastb

52. Which command limits the maximum number of processes a user can start?

A. ulimit -u

B. chmod

C. nice

D. sysctl -w

53. We want to audit all commands run by a user. Which tool is most appropriate?

A. acpid

B. auditd

C. atd

D. udevd

54. If a user is unable to use sudo due to "incorrect password," but their password works elsewhere, what is a possible cause?

A. /tmp is full

B. Network is down

C. Their user isn't in the sudoers file

D. SSH keys are expired

55. What is the default umask for newly created files for most users?

A. 0277

B. 0022

C. 0077

D. 0000

DOMAIN 5: Automation & Scripting

56. What Bash construct will test if a file exists and is not empty?

A. `[ -z file.txt ]`

B. `[ -s file.txt ]`

C. `test -d file.txt`

D. `if file.txt`

57. How can we ensure a Python script exits with a failure code if an exception occurs?

A. `break`

B. `raise` only

C. `exit 0`

D. `sys.exit(1)` in except block

58. In Bash, which variable gives the exit status of the previous command?

A. `$!`

B. `$0`

C. `$?`

D. `$$`

59. Which Ansible module installs system packages?

A. `ansible.builtin.copy`

B. `ansible.builtin.package`

C. `ansible.builtin.lineinfile`

D. `ansible.builtin.command`

60. To run a command every 30 minutes with systemd timers, which OnCalendar value should we use?

A. `*:*:00`

B. `*:0,30`

C. `hourly`

D. `*/30 * * * *`

61. What is the standard file extension for a Bash script?

A. `.bashrc`

B. `.py`

C. `.conf`

D. `.sh`

62. In a Bash script, which syntax runs "command" in the background?

A. `& command`

B. `bg command`

C. `command &`

D. `command &&`

63. Which is a valid way to define a variable in Bash?

A. `name="value"`

B. `$name = value`

C. `set name value`

D. `define name value`

64. What Ansible command will show exactly what will change, but not apply changes?

A. `ansible-playbook --diff`

B. `ansible-playbook --list-tasks`

C. `ansible --syntax-check`

D. `ansible-playbook --check`

65. To ensure a script can be sourced and used by another, what line is usually required at the top?

A. `source /etc/profile`

B. `#!/bin/bash`

C. `exec bash`

D. `chmod +x script.sh`

66. How do we pass a variable from a shell to a Python script?

A. `python3 -e VAR=foo script.py`

B. `export script.py VAR`

C. `python3 script.py "$VAR"`

D. `python3 script.py < $VAR`

67. Which tool will schedule a script to run at system boot on most Linux systems using modern service management?

A. `cron @reboot`

B. `atd`

C. `systemctl enable myscript.service`

D. `rc.local`

68. What is the effect of `set -e` in a Bash script?

A. Exits on first failed command

B. Sets environment variables

C. Expands aliases

D. Echoes each command

DOMAIN 6: Networking & Troubleshooting

69. What does the command `ip a` display?

A. Routing table

B. All IP addresses and interface details

C. Default gateway

D. ARP cache

70. Which command will display the current default route?

A. `ss -tuln`

B. `ip route`

C. `arp -a`

D. `hostname -I`

71. To test DNS resolution for a domain and get detailed answers, which command is best?

A. `dig <domain>`

B. `ip addr show`

C. `route -n`

D. `ifconfig`

72. If a service is listening on TCP port 8080, which command lists the process?

A. `netstat -i`

B. `lsof -u`

C. `arp -n`

D. `ss -ltnp | grep 8080`

73. What is the main configuration file for static network settings using NetworkManager?

A. `/etc/netplan/*.yaml`

B. `/etc/network/interfaces`

C. `/etc/NetworkManager/system-connections/`

D. `/etc/sysconfig/network-scripts/ifcfg-*`

74. Which command can test connectivity to a specific port and show if it is open?

A. `nc -zv <host> <port>`

B. `ss -rn`

C. `ping <host>`

D. `traceroute <host>`

75. What would we use to display all established TCP connections and their owning processes?

A. `ss -tnao`

B. `arp -e`

C. `hostnamectl`

D. `ping -a`

76. Which two commands can show we which process is using a particular port (choose two)?

A. `ss -ltnp`

B. `lsof -i :<port>`

C. `arping <ip>`

D. `grep <port> /etc/services`

77. Which tool can continuously monitor traffic on a network interface in real-time?

A. `iftop`

B. `ss -s`

C. `nmcli`

D. `hostname -f`

78. A system's DNS queries are timing out. Which configuration file is most likely misconfigured?

A. `/etc/hostname`

B. `/etc/resolv.conf`

C. `/etc/hosts`

D. `/etc/nsswitch.conf`

79. To permanently add a static route using netplan, which file should we edit?

A. `/etc/sysconfig/network`

B. `/etc/network/interfaces`

C. `/etc/netplan/*.yaml`

D. `/etc/rc.local`

80. Which command will display network interface statistics such as dropped packets and errors?

A. `hostname -I`

B. `ip -s link`

C. `ss -l`

D. `arp -a`

DOMAIN 7: Containers, Virtualization & Cloud

81. Which command lists all running Docker containers?

A. `docker images`

B. `docker run`

C. `docker ps`

D. `docker rm`

82. In a Dockerfile, what is the effect of the `CMD` instruction?

A. Copies files into the image

B. Sets file permissions

C. Sets the default command to run when the container starts

D. Installs packages

83. What is a benefit of running applications inside containers?

A. Consistent environment across development and production

B. Limited portability

C. Increased hardware costs

D. Reduced isolation

84. Which command starts a virtual machine in headless mode with VirtualBox?

A. `VBoxManage startvm <vmname> --type headless`

B. `virsh start <vmname>`

C. `qemu-system-x86_64 <image>`

D. `vagrant up`

85. When launching a cloud-init based VM, where are user-supplied configuration scripts usually stored?

A. `/etc/rc.local`

B. `/home/cloud-init`

C. `/root/userdata`

D. `/var/lib/cloud/instances/<id>/user-data.txt`

86. To see a full log of how cloud-init configured the VM, which file do we check?

A. `/home/ubuntu/init.log`

B. `/var/log/messages`

C. `/var/log/cloud-init-output.log`

D. `/etc/cloud-init.conf`

87. Which Docker Compose command brings up services in the background?

A. `docker compose run`

B. `docker compose stop`

C. `docker compose build`

D. `docker compose up -d`

88. What is the purpose of mapping a host directory to a container with `-v /data:/data`?

A. Limits the container's CPU usage

B. Upgrades the container's kernel

C. Persists data created by the container on the host

D. Installs a volume driver

89. In Kubernetes, what object is used to persist storage beyond pod lifecycles?

A. DaemonSet

B. PersistentVolumeClaim

C. ReplicaSet

D. ServiceAccount

90. What is the result of running `docker exec -it <container> bash`?

A. Pushes the image to the registry

B. Launches an interactive Bash shell inside the running container

C. Removes the container

D. Builds a new container

ANSWER KEY

1. A
2. D
3. C
4. C
5. C
6. C
7. B
8. A
9. B
10. B
11. B
12. C
13. D
14. B
15. A
16. D
17. B
18. B
19. D
20. C
21. A
22. A
23. C
24. C
25. A
26. B
27. B
28. A
29. A

30. B
31. C
32. C
33. D
34. A
35. B
36. C
37. D
38. D
39. C
40. B
41. C
42. A
43. B
44. A
45. D
46. B
47. B
48. B
49. D
50. C
51. A
52. A
53. B
54. C
55. B
56. B
57. D
58. C

59. B
60. B
61. D
62. C
63. A
64. D
65. B
66. C
67. C
68. A
69. B
70. B
71. A
72. D
73. C
74. A
75. A
76. A, B
77. A
78. B
79. C
80. B
81. C
82. C
83. A
84. A
85. D
86. C
87. D

88. C

89. B

90. B

MOCK EXAM

SET 'B'

DOMAIN 1: System Architecture & Installation

1. **Which command shows the running kernel version?**

   A. `lsmod`

   B. `uname -r`

   C. `cat /etc/issue`

   D. `lsb_release -a`

2. **On most modern Linux systems, what does runlevel 1 represent?**

   A. Multi-user with GUI

   B. Single-user (maintenance) mode

   C. Halt

   D. Reboot

3. **Which command displays available memory and swap usage?**

   A. `free -h`

   B. `df -h`

   C. `du -sh`

   D. `vmstat -d`

4. **We want to load a kernel module called `loop`. Which command will we use?**

   A. `insmod loop`

   B. `rmmod loop`

   C. `depmod -a`

   D. `modprobe loop`

5. **To view connected USB devices, which command is most suitable?**

   A. `lsusb`

   B. `lspci`

   C. `lsmod`

   D. `fdisk -l`

6. **Which file typically holds static kernel parameters for early boot?**

   A. `/etc/default/grub`

B. `/etc/modprobe.conf`

C. `/boot/grub/grub.cfg`

D. `/etc/fstab`

7. **What is the purpose of the `/etc/hosts` file?**

A. Set shell environment variables

B. Local hostname to IP resolution

C. Store default runlevel

D. Configure default user shell

8. **When we want to see which dynamic libraries a binary links to, which command helps?**

A. `ldd <binary>`

B. `modprobe <binary>`

C. `ls -lh <binary>`

A. `cat <binary>`

9. **Which package manager is native to Ubuntu?**

A. `zypper`

B. `yum`

C. `apt`

D. `dnf`

10. **Which directory contains files describing block devices in the kernel's device tree?**

A. `/etc/block/`

B. `/sys/block/`

C. `/dev/block/`

D. `/proc/block/`

11. **If we want to install all available updates, which command do we use?**

A. `apt update`

B. `apt-get install`

C. `apt full-upgrade`

D. `apt search`

12. **A user needs to switch to a graphical runlevel on a system using System V init. Which command would we use?**

    A. `init 3`

    B. `runlevel 1`

    C. `telinit 5`

    D. `systemctl isolate multi-user.target`

13. **What is the function of the `PATH` environment variable?**

    A. Lists default runlevel

    B. Directory search order for commands

    C. Sets the shell prompt

    D. User's home directory location

DOMAIN 2: System Configuration & Management

14. **Which command will change a user's primary group to `staff`?**

    A. `usermod -g staff <user>`

    B. `groupadd staff <user>`

    C. `passwd -g staff <user>`

    D. `chown -G staff <user>`

15. **Where would we look to verify the configuration for systemd service overrides?**

    A. `/etc/systemd/system/<service>.service.d/`

    B. `/etc/init.d/`

    C. `/usr/local/bin/`

    D. `/etc/default/`

16. **Which file lists groups a user belongs to?**

    A. `/etc/passwd`

    B. `/etc/shadow`

C. `/etc/group`

D. `/var/log/auth.log`

17. What tool configures system-wide time and NTP settings on modern systems?

A. `timedatectl`

B. `date`

C. `hwclock`

D. `ntpdate`

18. The main purpose of `/etc/nsswitch.conf` is to:

A. Control library path order

B. Specify sources for system databases

C. Configure file descriptor limits

D. Set default editor

19. Which command enables a service at boot with systemd?

A. `systemctl enable <service>`

B. `service <service> start`

C. `initctl enable <service>`

D. `chkconfig <service> on`

20. To see which users are currently logged in, which command do we use?

A. `last`

B. `users`

C. `who`

D. `uptime`

21. What is the effect of the `nologin` shell in `/etc/passwd`?

A. Prevents user logins

B. Disables the network

C. Enables root login

D. Launches a restricted shell

22. Which tool edits a user's crontab interactively?

A. `cronedit`

B. `crontab -e`

C. `at`

D. `nano /etc/crontab`

23. Where is the default system log configuration for rsyslog found?

A. `/etc/syslog.conf`

B. `/etc/rsyslog.conf`

C. `/var/log/messages`

D. `/etc/logrotate.conf`

24. Which command displays only the memory usage summary for running processes?

A. `ps aux`

B. `top`

C. `free`

D. `vmstat`

25. What is the output of `echo $HOME`?

A. Name of current shell

B. Home directory path

C. User's group name

D. System hostname

26. What command lists all environment variables for the current session?

A. `set`

B. `export`

C. `env`

D. `printenv`

27. To disable root SSH logins, which configuration do we change?

A. `/etc/ssh/ssh_config`

B. `/etc/ssh/sshd_config`

C. `/etc/securetty`

D. `/etc/shadow`

28. Which command reloads the systemd daemon after us create or edit a service file?

A. `systemctl daemon-reload`

B. `systemctl reload`

C. `systemctl restart`

D. `systemctl reset-failed`

DOMAIN 3: Storage & Filesystems

29. Which command initializes a new LVM volume group?

A. `mkfs.vg`

B. `pvcreate`

C. `vgcreate`

D. `lvcreate`

30. We want to view disk usage in a specific directory and its subdirectories. Which command is best?

A. `ls -l`

B. `du -sh *`

C. `df -h`

D. `fdisk -l`

31. If `/etc/fstab` contains an error and the system drops into rescue mode, what file should we edit to correct it?

A. `/etc/hosts`

B. `/etc/fstab`

C. `/etc/shadow`

D. `/etc/profile`

32. Which command will add a new ext4 filesystem on `/dev/sdb1`?

A. `mkfs.ext4 /dev/sdb1`

B. `fsck.ext4 /dev/sdb1`

C. `tune2fs /dev/sdb1`

D. `mount /dev/sdb1`

33. What mount option would make `/var` read-only?

A. `rw`

B. `exec`

C. `ro`

D. `defaults`

34. Which command displays UUIDs for all block devices?

A. `fdisk -l`

B. `lsblk -f`

C. `blkid`

D. `lsmod`

35. What command checks and repairs an XFS filesystem?

A. `xfs_check`

B. `xfs_repair`

C. `xfs_growfs`

D. `fsck.xfs`

36. To show all available free space in a volume group, which command do we use?

A. `pvscan`

B. `vgs`

C. `lvscan`

D. `vgdisplay`

37. Which entry in `/etc/fstab` mounts a swap partition at boot?

A. `/dev/sda2 swap swap defaults 0 0`

B. `/dev/sda2 / swap defaults 0 0`

C. `/dev/sda2 none swap sw 0 0`

D. `/dev/sda2 /mnt swap sw 0 0`

38. How can we check the consistency of an NFS mount from the client side?

A. `showmount -e`

B. `exportfs -v`

C. `mount -v`

D. `ls -l <mountpoint>`

39. If a filesystem is mounted with `noexec`, what will fail?

A. File reads

B. File writes

C. Executing binaries

D. Reading directory listings

40. Which command will immediately activate a swap partition?

A. `swapon <device>`

B. `swapctl <device>`

C. `activate swap <device>`

D. `mount -t swap <device>`

41. What tool grows an ext4 filesystem online (after LV resize)?

A. `resize2fs`

B. `mkfs.ext4`

C. `xfs_growfs`

D. `tune2fs`

DOMAIN 4: Security

42. What does the command `passwd -l bob` do?

A. Lists user details

B. Locks user bob

C. Changes bob's shell

D. Unlocks user bob

43. Which file controls password aging policy for all users?

A. `/etc/login.defs`

B. `/etc/hosts`

C. `/etc/shadow`

D. `/etc/security/pwpolicy.conf`

44. Which utility will show SELinux status and mode?

A. `getenforce`

B. `setsebool`

C. `semanage`

D. `sestatus`

45. If we want to audit every command a user runs, which system would we use?

A. `udevadm`

B. `auditd`

C. `dbus`

D. `cron`

46. To require users to change their password at next login, which command do we run?

A. `passwd -u <user>`

B. `chage -d 0 <user>`

C. `passwd -l <user>`

D. `useradd -e <date>`

47. Where are SSH authorized keys for user alice stored by default?

A. `/home/alice/.ssh/authorized_keys`

B. `/etc/ssh/sshd_config`

C. `/var/ssh/authorized_keys`

D. `/home/alice/.ssh/id_rsa`

48. Which command shows all open ports and listening services?

A. `ss -tuln`

B. `hostnamectl`

C. `last`

D. `lsmod`

49. What is the default location of the sudoers configuration file?

A. `/etc/sudoers`

B. `/usr/sbin/sudoers`

C. `/etc/shadow`

D. /usr/local/etc/sudoers

50. How can we lock a user out after three failed login attempts using PAM?

A. Edit /etc/pam.d/common-auth with pam_tally2

B. Set PermitRootLogin no in sshd_config

C. Add a cron job

D. Set shell to /bin/false

51. What does the `chmod 700 file.txt` command do?

A. Read, write, and execute only for owner

B. Read for all

C. Read/write for group

D. Execute for all

52. Which utility can view kernel audit logs?

A. ausearch

B. lslogins

C. loginctl

D. journalctl --user

53. Where is the main configuration file for the firewall?

A. /etc/firewalld/firewalld.conf

B. /etc/firewall.conf

C. /etc/nftables.conf

D. /etc/sysconfig/iptables

54. If we want to verify the fingerprint of an SSH host key, which command is best?

A. ssh-keygen -lf /etc/ssh/ssh_host_rsa_key.pub

B. cat /etc/ssh/ssh_config

C. finger

D. hostname

55. Which PAM module locks a user after too many failed logins?

A. pam_tally2

B. pam_login

C. `pam_env`

D. `pam_exec`

DOMAIN 5: Automation & Scripting

56. In Bash, how do we loop through every file ending with `.txt` in a directory?

A. `for f in *.txt; do ... done`

B. `for *.txt in dir; do ... done`

C. `while *.txt; do ... done`

D. `loop *.txt; do ... done`

57. Which line prints every line in a file containing "ERROR" using awk?

A. `awk '/ERROR/ {print $0}' file.log`

B. `awk 'ERROR' file.log`

C. `cat file.log | grep ERROR`

D. `sed 'ERROR' file.log`

58. What exit code in Bash typically indicates success?

A. 1

B. 2

C. 0

D. 255

59. Which file extension is conventional for Python scripts?

A. `.bash`

B. `.sh`

C. `.py`

D. `.ps`

60. How do we assign the output of a command to a variable in Bash?

A. `output=$(command)`

B. `output=command`

C. `$output=command`

D. `let output=command`

61. In Ansible, which module is best to copy a file to a remote host?

A. `copy`

B. `package`

C. `service`

D. `cron`

62. What does the cron schedule `0 2 * * 1` do?

A. Runs at 2am every Monday

B. Runs at 2pm daily

C. Runs at 2am on the first day of the month

D. Runs every minute

63. In Bash, what is the function of `shift` in a script?

A. Moves positional parameters left

B. Ends the script

C. Shifts variable values

D. Ignores errors

64. What does `set -u` in Bash do?

A. Treats unset variables as an error

B. Runs script in user mode

C. Unsets all variables

D. Updates the path

65. What command shows only the processes owned by the current user?

A. `ps -u $USER`

B. `ps aux | grep root`

C. `ps -ef`

D. `ps -a`

66. In a shell script, which shebang specifies to use Bash?

A. `#!/bin/bash`

B. `#!/usr/bin/python3`

C. `#!/bin/zsh`

D. `#!/usr/bin/env`

67. Which tool schedules a one-time task for the future?

A. `at`

B. `cron`

C. `systemd`

D. `timer`

68. What does the `trap` command in Bash do?

A. Catches and responds to signals

B. Schedules a task

C. Restarts a process

D. Sets a variable

DOMAIN 6: Networking & Troubleshooting

69. What command shows the routing table?

A. `ip route`

B. `arp -a`

C. `ifconfig -a`

D. `ip link`

70. Which command is used to look up the MX records of a domain?

A. `dig MX <domain>`

B. `traceroute <domain>`

C. `ifconfig <domain>`

D. `ping <domain>`

71. Which file should we edit to set a static IP with netplan?

A. `/etc/network/interfaces`

B. `/etc/netplan/*.yaml`

C. `/etc/hosts`

D. `/etc/hostname`

72. Which command shows current TCP connections by state?

A. `ss -ant`

B. `ping -c 1`

C. `host <ip>`

D. `arp -n`

73. A server's name does not resolve to its IP address. Which file would we check first for a local mapping?

A. `/etc/hosts`

B. `/etc/nsswitch.conf`

C. `/etc/resolv.conf`

D. `/etc/services`

74. To display all active network interfaces and addresses, which command do we use?

A. `ip a`

B. `arp -a`

C. `ifconfig -a`

D. `hostname -I`

75. How can we determine which process is using port 22?

A. `lsof -i :22`

B. `arping 22`

C. `ss -tunp | grep 22`

D. Both A and C

76. What does the `netstat -rn` command display?

A. Routing table

B. DNS cache

C. Network interface hardware addresses

D. Current hostname

77. Which command pings a remote host 5 times and then exits?

A. `ping -c 5 <host>`

B. `ping <host>`

C. `ping -t 5 <host>`

D. `arp <host>`

78. What file defines the search domains for DNS lookups?

A. `/etc/resolv.conf`

B. `/etc/hosts`

C. `/etc/named.conf`

D. `/etc/sysconfig/network`

79. Which tool captures and analyzes packets on a network interface?

A. `arping`

B. `tcpdump`

C. `ping`

D. `dig`

80. If a server cannot be pinged but services on it are reachable, what is a possible cause?

A. DNS server down

B. ICMP blocked by firewall

C. No route to host

D. Interface down

DOMAIN 7: Containers, Virtualization & Cloud

81. Which command creates a new Docker image from a Dockerfile?

A. `docker build -t myimage.`

B. `docker run myimage`

C. `docker exec myimage`

D. `docker compose up`

82. What is the primary function of Kubernetes?

A. Container orchestration

B. Virtual machine management

C. Network scanning

D. Static file serving

83. Which directory on a Linux system holds KVM virtual machine disk images by default?

A. `/home/vm`

B. `/var/lib/libvirt/images/`

C. `/usr/local/vm`

D. `/etc/kvm/`

84. Which Docker command displays resource usage stats for containers?

A. `docker top`

B. `docker logs`

C. `docker stats`

D. `docker inspect`

85. What is the effect of the `EXPOSE` instruction in a Dockerfile?

A. Publishes the port on the host

B. Documents a port for the container

C. Installs a network driver

D. Starts a web server

86. In cloud-init, which file contains the output from user-data scripts?

A. `/etc/cloud/cloud.cfg`

B. `/var/log/cloud-init-output.log`

C. `/root/cloud-init.log`

D. `/etc/init.d/cloud-init`

87. Which command shows all defined VMs in libvirt (KVM/QEMU)?

A. `virsh list --all`

B. `kvm --list`

C. `vmstat`

D. `virt-install --show`

88. To launch a container with a persistent data volume, which command is correct?

A. `docker run -v /data:/data busybox`

B. `docker build -v /data:/data busybox`

C. `docker exec -v /data:/data busybox`

D. `docker logs -v /data:/data busybox`

89. Which command will display logs for a running Docker container named `web`?

A. `docker top web`

B. `docker ps web`

C. `docker logs web`

D. `docker inspect web`

90. What is a primary benefit of using a cloud-init script during VM provisioning?

A. Automates initial configuration

B. Encrypts all disk volumes

C. Requires no SSH

D. Disables networking

ANSWER KEY

1. B
2. B
3. A
4. D
5. A
6. A
7. B
8. A
9. D
10. B
11. C
12. C
13. B
14. A
15. A

16. C
17. A
18. B
19. A
20. C
21. A
22. B
23. B
24. C
25. B
26. C
27. B
28. A
29. C
30. B
31. B
32. A
33. C
34. C
35. B
36. D
37. C
38. D
39. C
40. A
41. A
42. B
43. A
44. D

45. B

46. B

47. A

48. A

49. A

50. A

51. A

52. A

53. A

54. A

55. A

56. A

57. A

58. C

59. C

60. A

61. A

62. A

63. A

64. A

65. A

66. A

67. A

68. A

69. A

70. A

71. B

72. A

73. A

74. A

75. D

76. A

77. A

78. A

79. B

80. B

81. A

82. A

83. B

84. C

85. B

86. B

87. A

88. A

89. C

90. A

Index

V

W

X

Z

Epilogue

I'm really pleased to say that finishing this book and getting ready for the CompTIA Linux+ exam is a big deal. It's a clear sign that you're serious about growing as a Linux administrator and committed to building technical excellence. As you reach the end of this book and head towards exam day, it's only natural to start thinking about what's next. For a lot of people, Linux+ is a stepping stone to a wider range of job opportunities and more advanced certifications.

One of the best ways to get ahead is to get your hands on the CompTIA Security+ certification. It'll give you a good overall idea of network and system security, risk management, and how to handle incidents. With your Linux+ experience under your belt, you'll be all set to get to grips with security basics, handle authentication and authorisation, and get your head around implementing security best practices across various environments. If you're interested in administration at scale, the CompTIA Server+ and CompTIA Cloud+ certifications could be a great option for you. They'll give you the skills you need to get started in server and cloud management. They build on the system knowledge you get in Linux+, taking you deeper into topics like virtualisation, high availability, backup strategies and cloud orchestration.

But if you're keen to explore more specialised security roles, certifications like Certified Ethical Hacker (CEH), GIAC Security Essentials (GSEC) and even the Certified Information Systems Security Professional (CISSP) offer you a structured path into things like penetration testing, incident analysis and security architecture. Lots of professionals are getting into automation and infrastructure as code by getting certified in Red Hat (RHCSA, RHCE), Linux Foundation, or even DevOps toolsets like Ansible, Kubernetes, and Docker. With containers, cloud-native platforms, and scripting now a daily part of the job, these skills are in high demand.

As the landscape keeps on changing, the best administrators and engineers always keep learning. The skills you've picked up from working through scenario-driven recipes and practising problem-solving are going to be super useful as you grow. Every new system, network, and challenge is an opportunity to apply your skills and continue your journey.

Wherever you're headed next, keep asking questions, stay curious, and remember that being a Linux and open-source master is a journey that rewards those who go with the flow and are always looking to improve.

--Dorian Kelmor

Thank You

www.ingramcontent.com/pod-product-compliance
Lightning Source LLC
Chambersburg PA
CBHW080213170726
48282CB00030B/1097
9789349174276